APPLIED MEASUREMENT
WITH jMETRIK

jMetrik is a computer program for implementing classical and modern psychometric methods. It is designed to facilitate work in a production environment
and to make advanced psychometric procedures accessible to every measurement practitioner. *Applied Measurement with jMetrik* reviews psychometric theory
and describes how to use jMetrik to conduct a comprehensive psychometric
analysis. Each chapter focuses on a topic in measurement, describes the steps for
using jMetrik, and provides one or more examples of conducting an analysis on
the topic. Recommendations and guidance for practice are provided throughout
the book.

J. Patrick Meyer is an Associate Professor in the Curry School of Education at
the University of Virginia.

APPLIED MEASUREMENT WITH jMETRIK

J. Patrick Meyer

NEW YORK AND LONDON

First published 2014
by Routledge
711 Third Avenue, New York, NY 10017

and by Routledge
2 Park Square, Milton Park, Abingdon, Oxon, OX14 4RN

Routledge is an imprint of the Taylor & Francis Group, an informa business

© 2014 Taylor & Francis

Library of Congress Cataloging-in-Publication Data

Meyer, J. Patrick.
Applied measurement with jMetrik / by J. Patrick Meyer.
    pages cm
  Includes bibliographical references and index.
  1. Psychometrics—Data processing.   2. Psychological tests—Data processing.   3. jMetrik.   I. Title.
  BF176.2.M48   2014
  150.285'53—dc23

ISBN: 978-0-415-53195-5 (hbk)
ISBN: 978-0-415-53197-9 (pbk)
ISBN: 978-0-203-11519-0 (ebk)

Typeset in Bembo
by Apex CoVantage, LLC

Printed and bound in the United States of America by Publishers Graphics, LLC on sustainably sourced paper.

For Amelie, Aidan, and Christina

CONTENTS

FIGURES AND TABLES

Figures

Tables

PREFACE

jMetrik is a computer program for implementing classical and modern psychometric methods. It is designed to facilitate work in a production environment and to make advanced psychometric procedures accessible to every measurement practitioner. jMetrik combines data management capabilities and a wide array of psychometric procedures into a single program. This design improves productivity by reducing the amount of time you spend reshaping data and preparing syntax for an analysis. jMetrik's interface is user-friendly and makes it easy for measurement professionals to conduct an analysis. New and experienced practitioners can quickly run an analysis through the point-and-click menus, or they can automate an analysis through jMetrik commands. In this way, jMetrik scales to the experience of the user.

jMetrik focuses on established psychometric procedures that are commonly employed in operational testing programs. In its current state, jMetrik includes classical item analysis, reliability estimation, test scaling, differential item functioning, nonparametric item response theory, Rasch measurement models, and item response theory scale linking and score equating. In addition to psychometric methods, it offers a variety of statistical procedures such as frequencies, descriptive statistics, and density estimation. It also offers an array of charts and graphs for illustrating data.

On the data management side, jMetrik features an integrated database that allows users to easily organize and manipulate data. There is virtually no limit to the sample size or number of tables that can be stored in the database; users are only limited by the amount of storage on their computer. After importing data into jMetrik, users can create subsets of data by selecting examinees or variables. Users can also create new tables by saving the results of an analysis to the database for further processing.

The idea for jMetrik arose from two needs: (a) a need for a single program that could perform multiple psychometric procedures in a user-friendly way and (b) a need for a tool that helps students learn the practice of measurement. When I was in graduate school, a comprehensive analysis required multiple programs that were not designed to work with each other. You had one program for data management, another program for item analysis, a third program for item response theory, and a fourth program for linking and equating. Each of these programs had its own command syntax and required data in a different format. You would spend an excessive amount of time preparing data and syntax for an analysis. Moreover, the risk of human error was tremendous given all of the ways a mistake could happen. jMetrik aims to streamline the process for conducting a comprehensive analysis by providing a single data structure, user interface, and command structure for a wide variety of methods. The benefits of this approach are increased work efficiency and a reduction in the risk for human error. It also has the benefit of facilitating instruction.

As anyone who has taught a measurement course knows, it can easily digress into a course on psychometric software. Students new to measurement get confused by the data structures and command syntax required by various programs. Consequently, class time that should be spent teaching measurement theory is sacrificed for time needed to teach software. The integrated and user-friendly nature of jMetrik overcomes this problem. Students quickly learn to use jMetrik after a short demonstration. This ease-of-use allows instructors to spend more time teaching measurement theory. Students ultimately get more out of the course because they learn more theory and gain more practice with measurement procedures.

This book is based on notes from an online short course that I have been teaching since the release of jMetrik version 2. Like the workshop, the purpose of this book is to describe psychometric methods available in jMetrik and explain the way to implement them with the software. Each chapter begins with a description of the method in enough detail for the reader to understand the options available in jMetrik. This material is not a comprehensive treatment of each subject. It is only introductory/review material that is intended to complement information from more exhaustive and theoretical measurement textbooks. The introductory section of each chapter is followed by a section that describes the options available in jMetrik and the steps for conducting an analysis. Each chapter ends with one or more demonstrations of an analysis that you can reproduce with the software and example data files.

Target Audience

This book is intended for students and professionals wishing to learn more about jMetrik and psychometrics. It requires a basic understanding of statistical concepts such as descriptive statistics, correlation and regression, and hypothesis testing. Any concepts that go beyond this basic level are explained in the book so that the reader can follow along and implement the procedures with jMetrik. This book can be used as a textbook or supplemental textbook for courses in measurement and psychometrics. The chapters on item analysis, reliability analysis and differential item functioning are suitable for an introductory course in measurement at the undergraduate or graduate level. Chapters on Rasch measurement, polytomous item response models, and scaling and linking are more advanced and would be suitable for an advanced undergraduate or intermediate graduate course in psychometrics. Regardless of your level of experience with psychometrics or your knowledge of measurement, this book will help you learn to use jMetrik to implement a variety of methods that are commonly found in a comprehensive psychometric analysis.

How to Obtain the Software

jMetrik is an open source application that is available free of charge from www. ItemAnalysis.com. It is a pure Java application that is compatible with 32- and 64-bit versions of Windows, Mac OSX, and Linux operating systems. It requires at least version 6 of the Java Runtime Environment (JRE). You can download the software with or without the required JRE. If you know that you have the correct version of the JRE, then use the installer that does not include it. It will download faster and require less storage space on your computer. If you do not have the correct version of Java or you are unsure, download the installer that includes the required JRE.

You have two options for the type of installer that you can download. The automated installer file will guide you through the installation process. This is the recommended approach, but it requires administrator privileges on most computers. The second option is an archive file installer (e.g. zip, tgz) that contains the application and supporting files. If you do not have administrator privileges, then try this second option and extract the files to a location where you have read/write permissions. After installation, start the program by double clicking the jMetrik icon.

jMetrik is quickly evolving as a program. Each new release includes new features, bug fixes, and refinements. The step-by-step instructions, interface screenshots, and output displays in this book are for version 3.1 of the software. There are not likely to be any major changes to the software features presented in this book, but small changes may occur. For example, a new version of jMetrik may show a button in a dialog that was not shown in this book. Major changes to the software will mainly involve new features, not major revisions to existing features. Major releases occur once or twice each year. jMetrik will inform you of new releases as they become available. You will need to repeat the steps for downloading and installing the software with each new release. Your databases and their data will be preserved when you install a new version.

How to Download the Example Data Files

All of the data files needed to follow the examples in this book are available for download from www.itemanalysis.com/example-data.php. They are stored in an archive file (i.e. zip, tar) that you must extract to a location on your computer. Each example data file is accompanied by a README file that provides information about the data file such as the answer key and example scoring syntax.

jMetrik Interface Orientation

Figure 0.1 shows the jMetrik interface. The main menu appears at the top of the interface. It includes options for File, Edit, Log, Manage, Transform, Analyze, Graph, Commands, and Help. Click one of the menu items to expand the menu and see more choices. Just beneath the main menu is the toolbar. This part of the interface provides quick access to some of the frequently used options in the main menu. It also provides access to functions not found in the main menu. In particular, the last two icons on the toolbar provide (a) information about the program's memory usage and (b) a quick way to close all tabs. One the left side of the interface, just beneath the toolbar is the table list. It shows data tables in the open database. To the right of the table list is a display of data. When you click a table name in the table list, it displays the data in the data view. The status bar is located along the bottom of the interface. It has three sections. The left section contains a description of the program's state, such as its current activity and error messages.

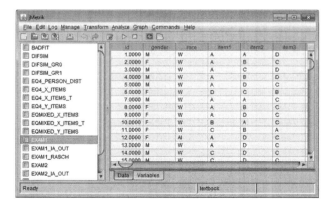

FIGURE 0.1 jMetrik graphical user interface

The middle section of the status bar displays the name of the open database. The right section contains a progress bar that shows the progress of an analysis.

Conventions for Referencing jMetrik Components

jMetrik uses a variety of dialogs and interface components to obtain your input and configure options for an analysis. Figure 0.2 shows an example of a dialog with the types of components you will encounter when using jMetrik. The dialog name appears on the title bar in the top left section of the dialog. In this example, the title is "Example," and the dialog itself includes six panels named: Select One Option, Select All That Apply, List Options, Input Options, Button Examples, and Text Area Input. In describing jMetrik options and the steps for conducting an analysis, I refer to interface components with the following conventions. Components are referenced by listing the component name and the component type in italics. The component name uses the name as it appears in the interface but the component type is always listed in lower case letters. For example, the *Select One Option panel* includes two radio buttons. The first button is named "Default option" and the second is named "Another radio button." The selected option in this panel is the *Default option radio button.* As implied by the name for this panel, you can select only one radio button in the same panel; the options are mutually exclusive. As a second example of the naming conventions, the *Select All That Apply panel* includes two checkboxes. The first checkbox is titled "Checkbox example" and the second is titled "Another option." Checkboxes are not mutually exclusive. You can select any, all, or none of them. In this example, the *Another option checkbox* is selected.

The *List Options panel* of the *Example dialog* in Figure 0.2 shows an example of a list. Database names and variable names are frequently presented in such a list. It is often necessary to refer to a specific variable in a list or some part of the

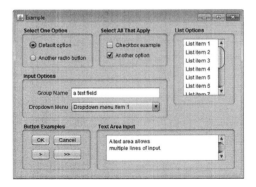

FIGURE 0.2 Example dialog and interface components

jMetrik output. To distinguish specific variables from the body of the text, they are written in a courier font. For example, `item1` refers to the variable named "item1" in a database.

The *Input Options panel* shows a text field and a drop-down menu. A text field allows a single line of input. In Figure 0.2, the *Group Name text field* contains the text "a text field." Like a set of radio buttons, a drop-down menu lists multiple items, but you can only choose one. The selected item appears in the collapsed view of the drop-down menu.

The *Button Examples panel* includes four buttons that are similar to ones you will see in jMetrik. Buttons perform actions that are indicated by their name. For example, the *OK button* is one you press to accept your selections and close a dialog. The button actions are not always evident in their name. For example, last two buttons listed in the *Button Examples panel* are named ">" and ">>", and they are commonly seen in jMetrik. The button ">" is referred to as a *Select button*, and the button ">>" is referred to as a *Select All button*. If the arrows on these buttons are pointing the other way, they have the opposite meaning. For example, a button named "<" is an *Unselect button*, and a button named "<<" is referred to as an *Unselect All button*.

Finally, the *Text Area Input panel* shows an example of a text area. Unlike a text field, a text area allows for multiple lines of input. These are less common in jMetrik, but when you see one, know that you can enter multiple lines of text.

The jMetrik Log and Running Commands

All commands and error messages are recorded in the jMetrik log. You can view the current state of the log by clicking **Log → View Log**. The displayed text file shows only the current state of the log. It does not automatically update once it is open. You must repeat these steps to see the most up-to-date information in the log. The log is a useful way to keep a record of your analysis. You can save the log as a plain text file, but you must save it before you close jMetrik. The log is cleared each time you start the program.

Every process in jMetrik has a corresponding command that is written to the log when you execute an analysis. Use the log to view these commands. You cannot run commands directly from the log because it may contain error messages and other information that is not a command. However, you can copy the commands from the log and paste them into a new text file for replicating an analysis. With the command text file open, click **Commands → Run Command** to run all of the commands in the text file.

ACKNOWLEDGMENTS

I would like to thank Melissa Berry, Margaret Ann Bollmeier, and the Curry School Foundation for their support with the production of jMetrik workshops and online short courses. Those events gave rise to the content of this book, and none of it would have been possible without their help and encouragement. I would also like to Xiaoxin Wei for her help in reviewing the examples in this book and providing feedback on earlier drafts. The content of this book benefitted from her feedback. Any remaining mistakes are my own. Finally, I would like to thank everyone who is using jMetrik. Your involvement with the software keeps the project alive, and your feedback helps ensure a productive user experience.

1

DATA MANAGEMENT

A relational database management system (RDBMS) lies at the heart of jMetrik, and it is responsible for all of jMetrik's data management capabilities. An RDBMS allows data and information about the data to be stored in multiple tables rather than a single flat file. This feature increases the efficiency of the program and provides a common framework for all data sets. You can think of jMetrik as a simplified interface to the RDBMS that gives you easy access to the most essential procedures for data management. You can import and export data, select subsets of data, and delete variables or an entire table. jMetrik organizes data management into three types of operations: database operations, table operations, and variable operations. This chapter begins with a description of the default RDBMS and naming conventions enforced by jMetrik. It then describes all three types of database operations and gives step-by-step instructions for data management features in jMetrik. It also describes noteworthy limitations to data management and provides recommendations for best practices.

Default RDBMS

Apache Derby is the default RDBMS in jMetrik (see http://db.apache.org/derby/). Much of the following information is specific to Derby and is subject to change if you use jMetrik with another RBDMS. Like jMetrik, Derby is a pure Java application that is compatible with any operating system. It stores data in a platform independent manner allowing you to move a database from one computer to another without affecting your ability to work with the database. Even if the Derby database is created with a Windows computer, the data are readable by a Linux or Mac OSX machine.

There is virtually no limit to the number of tables in a Derby database and virtually no limit to the number of cases (i.e. number of examinees) in a table—"virtually no limit" because the actual limit is the size of your computer's hard drive. Almost all modern computers are built with more than enough storage. You are unlikely to reach this limit in practice. The main limitation to consider is that each table is limited to 1,024 variables. If your data file has more than this number of variables, you should separate it into multiple tables. It is also good practice to use data files with far fewer than the maximum number of variables because some jMetrik procedures will add variables to the table. jMetrik will produce an error if you try to add a variable to a table that already contains the maximum number of variables. jMetrik only works with the default RDBMS as of this writing. Functionality for other RDBMSs will be added in the future.

Database Home

Through the RDBMS you create a database that contains any number of tables, and each table may contain one or more variables. You only need one database to store all of your tables, but you may find it easier to use multiple databases to organize your data. For example, you could create one database to store all of your math test data and another database to store all of your science test data. jMetrik allows you to easily switch between databases, but you can only access one database at a time. This restriction means that you should keep all of the tables that you need for an analysis in the same database. Think of each database as an independent entity. You cannot combine data or analysis methods across multiple databases.

Databases are stored on a computer's hard drive in a folder referred to as the database home. By default, this location is a subfolder of the user's home folder. For example, on a Windows machine the default location is C:\Users\<user name>\jmetrik\databases. You may view the current location of databases on your computer through the *jMetrik Preferences dialog*. Click **Edit → Preferences** to display this dialog. Your databases are stored in the folder listed in the *Home text field* of the *Database Options panel*. This location will be ideal for most people, but you can change it through the preferences dialog. The only restriction is that you must have read/write permissions on the folder where the databases are stored. If you change the database home, you will be prompted to restart jMetrik.

One reason why you may want to change the database home is if you are working with a team of researchers and you are sharing a database. One team member can create the database on a shared resource to make it accessible by everyone on the team. Each person can set the shared resource as the database home and work on the same database. However, only one person can access the database at a time. jMetrik does not allow multiple people to simultaneously access the same database.

Organizing Data in jMetrik and Table Descriptions

Given that a database will contain numerous tables, you should develop a table naming strategy to help you quickly remember the contents of each table. For example, you could concatenate two-digit codes that reflect the grade, subject, and year of an academic test. With this convention, a table named g3ma11 would contain data for the grade 3 math test given in 2011, and a table named g3ma12 would contain data for the following year. jMetrik lists tables in alphabetical order. To keep related tables next to each other in the list, your naming strategy for output tables should make use of the underscore character and extend from your original table name. For example, the item analysis output table for the grade 3 math 2011 test could be labeled g3ma11_iaout. The Rasch models analysis output table could be named g3ma11_rasch. Following these conventions, analysis of subsets could extend the table name again. An item analysis of the grade 3 math 2011 test for females could be named g3ma11 _female_iaout, and the analysis for males could be g3ma11 _male_iaout. It is entirely up to you to choose a naming convention, but a systematic method for naming tables in jMetrik will help you keep the information organized and identify table contents by only using the name.

In addition to a naming convention, jMetrik allows you to provide a written description of each table to help you keep track of table contents. jMetrik automatically provides a minimal description for any table created in jMetrik. You can edit this information and provide more details about a table or record other notes about the table for later reference. The description is limited to 1,000 characters, and you can edit it at any time through the *Table Descriptions dialog.* To start the dialog, click **Manage** → **Table Descriptions**. Select the table in the list on the left side of the dialog, and then add or edit a description in the text area. Press the *Submit button* to save your description. You can continue writing descriptions by selecting another table. Press the *Submit button* after adding or editing a description. Press the *OK button* when you are done to close the dialog and return to the main program. Make heavy use of table descriptions because your database will eventually contain hundreds of tables. Table descriptions will help you keep track of them and make it easier to recollect table contents.

The following sections discuss three types of data management operations that you can perform: database operations, table operations, and variable operations.

Database Operations

After you install jMetrik, you must create a database to hold your data. You only need to create one database, but you can create others if it helps to organize your data. To create a database, click **Manage** → **New Database**, and type a name for the database in the dialog. Click the *Create button* to produce the database, or click *Cancel* to return to the program.

TABLE 1.1 Naming conventions in jMetrik

Database Structure	Permitted Characters	Case Sensitive[a]	Maximum Length
Database	A–Z, 0–9, _	No	System
Table	A–Z, 0–9, _	No	120
Variable	A–Z, 0–9, _	No	20

[a]Although names are not case sensitive, you should only use names with all lowercase letters.

The name you choose for a database must comply with the following conventions and recommendations. Database names are case insensitive, meaning that the name "mydb" and the name "myDB" are equal in the eyes of the program. jMetrik will convert all database names to lower case. You can use the letters A through Z and the digits 0 through 9 in a database name. White spaces and punctuation marks are prohibited from database names. jMetrik will attempt to remove white spaces and punctuation marks from a database name before creating a database. It will inform you of any changes it makes to the database name. For the default RDBMS, there is virtually no limit to the length of a database name. However, good practice dictates the use of short yet descriptive database names. Database names longer than 120 characters are cumbersome to read in jMetrik and are not recommended. Table 1.1 summarizes database, table, and variable naming conventions.

Creating a database adds files to your computer and makes the database available to jMetrik, but it does not open the database. You must open a database before you begin using it. Click **Manage** → **Open Database**, and select the database that you would like to open in the dialog. Click the *OK button* to open the database. Once it is open, you will see the database name appear in the middle section of the status bar, and a list of existing tables will be displayed in the list on the left side of the interface. If the database is new and no tables have been created, nothing will be listed in the interface. You must import data into jMetrik to create a table and make data available to the program.

A database will remain available to the program until it is deleted. Once you no longer need a database, you can delete it by clicking **Manage** → **Delete Database** to display the *Delete Database dialog*. Select the database you would like to delete from the list of available databases, and then click the *Delete button*. You will be warned before any action is taken. If you accept the warning, your database will be permanently deleted from the system. Be very careful when you choose to delete a database. It is not possible to recover the database after it has been deleted.

Table Operations

Table operations in jMetrik give you control over importing, exporting, and deleting tables in the database. There is also an operation for viewing and editing table descriptions. To begin using a data file, you must first import it into jMetrik.

Importing Data

You can import a comma, tab, colon, or semicolon delimited file that contains no more than 1,024 variables. A delimited file may have variable names in the first row that uniquely identify each column of data. Variable names must be unique values that are 20 characters or less. They are limited to the characters A through Z, the numbers 0 through 9, and the underscore character "_". White spaces and punctuation marks are not allowed in variable names and will be automatically removed by jMetrik. As a recommended practice, use an underscore to represent a space in your variable name. For example, you could represent the variable "student id" as "student_id." Variable names are case insensitive, meaning that the variable "student_ID" and the variable "student_id" are viewed as the same value by the program. However, it is recommended that you use all variable names with letters in the same case (i.e. all lowercase or all uppercase). If your delimited file does not include variable names in the first row, jMetrik will create unique generic names (e.g. V1, V2, V3) and add them to the data table during import.

To import data into an open database, click **Manage** → **Import Data** to display the *Import Data dialog* (not shown). Type a name for your table in the first text field. Table names must be unique to a database, and they are limited to the letters A through Z, the digits 0 through 9, and the underscore character, "_". Table names must be 120 characters or less, and they must start with a letter. White spaces and punctuation marks are prohibited and will be eliminated by jMetrik prior to creating a table. The program will inform you of any changes to your table name.

After typing a name for the database, click the *Browse button* to display the *Import File selector* (see Figure 1.1). Use the *Import File selector* to find and select the delimited file you wish to import. The selector only shows you the names of plain

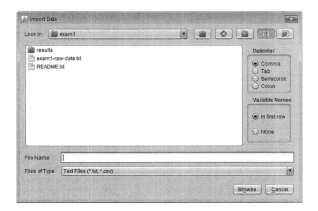

FIGURE 1.1 Import File selector

text (★.txt) and common delimited (★.csv) files by default. You can have it show you all files by selecting this option in the *Files of Type drop-down menu*.

The *Import File selector* contains two additional options that affect the import behavior. The *Delimiter panel* allows you to select the type of delimiter in the data file. The default delimiter is a comma, but you can select any of the other three types of delimiters in this panel (i.e. semicolon, colon, or tab). The *Variable Names panel* allows you to specify whether the delimited file contains variable names in the first row of data or not. Variables names are assumed to be in the first row of your file by default. If the delimited file contains variable names, these names must comply with the variable name restrictions described earlier.

Choose the delimiter and variable name options carefully. If you make the wrong selections, your data will not import properly. A frequent mistake is to select the *In First Row radio button* when your data file does not actually include variable names in the first row. jMetrik usually generates an error when this happens because it reads the first row of data as variables names, but the first row of data does not contain unique values. If your data file does not include variable names, be sure to select the *None radio button* in the *Variable Names panel*. After you select the appropriate options and choose your delimited file, click the *Browse button* to accept your selections and return to the *Import Data dialog*.

If you would like to add a table description for your data file, type it in the *Description text area*. You are limited to 1,000 characters. If you do not provide a description during the import process, jMetrik will add one for you that includes the path and filename of the imported file. You can always edit this description later through the *Table Descriptions dialog*.

To execute the import process, click the *Import button*. Depending on the size of your file, the import could take anywhere from a few seconds to a few minutes. For each data file that you import into jMetrik, the software will create two database tables. One table contains the data, and another table contains information about the variables in the table. The jMetrik interface displays information from these two tables in the *Data tab* and the *Variables tab*, respectively. The *Data tab* only provides a view of the data. It is there to help you verify that data imported correctly and to see the data contained in each variable. jMetrik does not allow you to edit the data directly. You can edit information in the *Variables tab* either directly or through dialogs that are explained in the chapter on item scoring.

To demonstrate the import procedures, use the exam1.txt data file that you can download from www.ItemAnalysis.com. Type "exam1" (without quotes) as the table name, and click the *Browse button* to start the *Import File selector*. Use the *Import File selector* to navigate to the exam1.txt file on your computer and select it. It is a comma delimited file with variable names in the first row. Therefore, use the default options in the *Import File selector*. Click the *Browse button* to close the selector, and then click the *Import button* to execute the import. Imported data will be displayed in the *Data tab* after a successful import. Now that your data are imported, you can run frequencies and descriptive statistics on the data or create various plots of the data. You cannot use any of the psychometric procedures until you conduct item scoring as described in the next chapter.

Importing Files with Missing Data

During the import process, jMetrik will convert a missing value into a null value in the database. In order for this conversion to take place, you must tell jMetrik how to identify missing data. You have several ways to tell jMetrik about your missing data. You can (a) exclude a response from your data file, (b) use a white space[1] to represent missing data, or (c) use the code "NA" (without quotes) to indicate missing data. All of these values will be converted to a null value during import. The codes will not be part of the data after an import.

For example, suppose a data set has five variables (ID, V1, V2, V3, V4) and the second examinee (EX2) is missing a value for V3. If you exclude a response to indicate missing data, a comma delimited file would appear as

```
ID,V1,V2,V3,V4
EX1,1,0,0,1
EX2,1,1,,0
EX3,0,0,1,0
```

Notice that for EX2 there is no value for V3 as indicated by the consecutive commas (i.e. ",,"). Alternatively, you could also use a white space to denote missing data. IBM® SPSS® uses this convention when creating a comma delimited file.[2] In this case, the previous example would appear as follows:

```
ID,V1,V2,V3,V4
EX1,1,0,0,1
EX2,1,1, ,0
EX3,0,0,1,0
```

Finally, the special code "NA" could be included in the data file. This convention is typical of the write.table and write.csv functions in R (R Core Team, 2013) when creating a delimited file. A data file that uses NA to indicate missing data would appear as follows:

```
ID,V1,V2,V3,V4
EX1,1,0,0,1
EX2,1,1,NA,0
EX3,0,0,1,0
```

All three methods are a global treatment of missing data. They will all be converted to a null value during the import process. The only way to undo this action is to delete the data table, change the code, and import the data again.

Treatment of Missing Data during an Analysis

Missing data occurs when an examinee does not have a value for a variable in the data. This pattern may be observed for multiple examinees and multiple variables in the data set. Missing data are problematic because no one knows the real values of the missing data. Assumptions are needed to substitute a value for missing data. The most basic assumption is that data are missing completely at random. In this case, data are missing by chance alone. Missingness (the absence of some responses for an examinee) is unrelated to any other variables in the data set. We have the most options for handling missing data when they are missing completely at random. Listwise deletion, pairwise deletion, and multiple imputation methods all result in unbiased estimates when data are missing completely at random. jMetrik offers an option for listwise deletion for some methods. If an examinee is missing a value for any variable included in an analysis, all of the examinee's data will be excluded from the analysis under listwise deletion. If you wish to preserve as much of an examinee's data as possible while excluding missing data, use the pairwise deletion option when available. This option will only exclude missing data for the smallest subset (e.g. a pair of variables) of data possible and preserve the remaining data. Unfortunately, missing completely at random is a very untenable assumption. It is not likely to be true for real data. Therefore, be extremely cautious when using listwise or pairwise deletion. It could result in biased estimates.

Missing at random is a second type of missing data assumption, and it is the more tenable assumption in practice. When data are missing at random, missingness is related to other variables in the data set but not related to the particular values that are missing. Listwise deletion and pairwise deletion methods produce biased estimates when data are missing at random. Other methods are required to overcome this limitation. Maximum likelihood and multiple imputation methods are two methods for handling missing data when data are missing at random. jMetrik does not provide tools for multiple imputation, but it does allow for maximum likelihood treatment of missing data when using item response theory (IRT). If a user chooses to ignore missing data when using IRT features in jMetrik, estimation will involve all available data.

Missing at random is the most likely missing data mechanism in practice, but a third type of missing data is also possible. When data are missing not at random, the missing values are the reason for being missing. That is, to know why data are missing, you must know what is missing—a seemingly impossible feat. As an example, suppose a survey asks for a respondent to report his income. If everyone who earns more than $500,000 does not answer the question, then the data are missing not at random. Handling data that are missing not at random is complicated and beyond the capabilities of jMetrik.

Subsetting Cases

During a comprehensive psychometric analysis, you may need to run an analysis on different subgroups. jMetrik allows you to create a new table that is a subset of an existing table. For example, the exam1 data contains demographics for gender and race. Gender groups include male (M) and female (F) examinees. Race groups include students from white (W), black or African American (B), Asian (A), and American Indian (AI) backgrounds. To create a subset of cases, click **Manage** → **Subset Cases** to open the *Subset Cases dialog* (see Figure 1.2). You will see a list of variable names on the left side of this dialog. Across the top of the dialog is a text area that allows you to specify the condition for the subset. You can type operators (e.g. =, <, AND) into this area directly, or you can press one of the buttons shown in the dialog to add an operator to the text area. Near the bottom of the dialog is a text field for typing a table name for the new table that will be created.

Figure 1.2 shows the *Subset Cases dialog* with a condition that defines a subset as anyone with a code of 'F' for gender (i.e. females). A table named exam1_female will be created once the *OK button* is pressed. In order to create your own subsets of cases, you must understand the subset syntax. An SQL WHERE clause lies at the heart of the subset cases feature in jMetrik. Any condition that you write must comply with the SQL-92 standard for a WHERE clause. A WHERE clause with a single condition is written with three elements: variable name, operator, and value. Variable names must exist in the table, and acceptable operators are defined by the RDBMS system (see Table 1.2). You provide the values that complete the condition. In the condition gender = 'F', the word "gender" is a variable name, the equals sign is the operator, and the letter F is the value. The letter

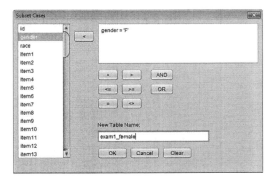

FIGURE 1.2 Subset Cases dialog

TABLE 1.2 WHERE statement operators and descriptions

Operator	Description
>	Greater than
<	Less than
=	Equal to
>=	Greater than or equal to
<=	Less than or equal to
<>	Not equal to
AND	Logical conjunction of two conditions; true only if both conditions are true
OR	Logical disjunction of two conditions; true if either condition is true

F is enclosed in single quotes because the variable gender contains text values. As another example, the condition `sumscore > 10` would create a subset of cases that includes examinees that score higher than 10 points. In this condition, "sumscore" is the variable name, > is the operator, and 10 is the value. The value 10 does not need to be in single quotes because sumscore contains numeric data. Be careful about writing your subset condition. jMetrik does not check the correctness of your syntax. If you accidentally omit the single quotes for text-based variables or mistype a variable name, jMetrik will produce an error without giving you any explanation.

If you have more than one condition, each condition must be separated by the AND or OR operator. Two conditions separated by the AND operator evaluate as true only if the first and second condition are true. For example, the WHERE clause `gender = 'M' AND race = 'W'` evaluates to true for white (`race='W'`) males (`gender='M'`), and your subset will only contain white males. If you have more than two conditions joined with the AND operator, the WHERE clause evaluates to true only if all conditions are true. For example, the WHERE clause `gender = 'M' AND race = 'W' AND sumscore > 10` evaluates to true for white (`race='W'`) males (`gender='M'`) that have a sumscore value greater than 10 points.

If you would like to create a subset of cases that contain examinees meeting any of two or more conditions provided in a WHERE clause, use the OR operator. Two conditions separated by the OR operator evaluate as true if either condition is true. It evaluates to false only when neither condition is true. For example, the WHERE clause `gender = 'M' OR race = 'W'` evaluates to true for white (`race='W'`) or male (`gender='M'`) examinees. Applying this subset criteria to the exam1 data results in a file that contains white male, white female, black male, Asian male, or American Indian male examinees. That is, it excludes any female examinees that are not white. Use of the AND and OR operators can be tricky. Be sure to view the new data table to check that you correctly defined your subset criteria. If you need help with writing a subset condition or would like to see more examples of acceptable WHERE clauses, search the internet for "SQL WHERE clause"; you will find numerous resources and examples.

Subsetting Variables

You have two options for selecting a subset of variables. The first method is to simply delete unwanted variables from your table. Select the table that contains the unwanted variables. Click **Manage** → **Delete Variables** to display the *Delete Variables dialog*. Select all of the variables you would like to delete, and press the *Run button*. You will be asked to confirm your decision to delete the variables. Press the *OK button*, and the variables will be deleted. You cannot undo this action. Deleting a variable permanently removes it from the table. The second option for subsetting variables is safer and does not affect the original table in jMetrik.

You can create a new table that contains a subset of variables from the original table. Select the table that contains the variables of interest. Click **Manage** → **Subset Variables** to display the *Variable Subset dialog*. Choose the variable you would like to have included in the new table. Type a name for the new table in the *New Table Name text field*, and press the *OK button*. A new table containing the selected variables will appear in the list of tables once it has been created. In addition, jMetrik will create a variable table with a copy of the scoring information. There is no need to repeat the scoring process for tables created in this manner.

Exporting Data

Exporting data is just the opposite of importing it. Data stored in a table in jMetrik are converted to a delimited plain text file and saved to your hard drive. Two of the options for an export are the same as the import options, but two others are new. To start the *Export Data dialog*, click **Manage** → **Export Data**. Along the right side of the dialog, you will see a panel for the *Delimiter option* and a panel for the *Variable Names option*. These have the same function as described earlier for importing data. The *Option panel* shows two new options. Selecting the *Scored Items checkbox* will cause jMetrik to export scored item responses instead of the original raw data. Choosing the *Use Quotes checkbox* will force jMetrik to enclose all values in double quotes. It is good to use this option if you have data that contain white spaces and you need to preserve this information when the exported file is read by another program. jMetrik populates the file location and file name for you, but you can edit this information as needed. Click the *OK button* to complete the export.

Deleting Database Tables

You have two options for deleting a table from the database. To delete a single table, select it in the table list, and press the delete key on a PC (fn + Delete on a

Mac). You will be asked to confirm the deletion. Press the *OK button* to continue with the delete. Be very sure you no longer need the table before you delete it. You cannot recover a table once it has been deleted.

The second method for deleting a table actually allows you to delete multiple tables at the same time. Click **Manage → Delete Table** to display the *Delete Table dialog* and see a list of all tables in the database. Select a single table by clicking it. You can select multiple tables by holding the Ctrl key while selecting each table. Press the *OK button* to continue with the delete, and then confirm your choice in the subsequent dialog. If you choose to delete tables, your choice is permanent. You cannot recover deleted tables.

Variable Operations

Variable operations include functions for renaming variables. To rename a variable, click the *Variables tab*, and then double click on a variable name to display the *Rename Variable dialog*. Type a new name for the variable, and press the *OK button* to rename the variable. jMetrik will modify your new name if necessary to make it comply with the naming conventions described earlier. If you attempt to use a name that already exists in the table, the variable will not be renamed, and jMetrik will produce an error message.

You can also use the subset variables process to create a copy of a table. All you need to do is select all variables for the new table. For example, to copy exam1, select the exam1 table in the list. Click **Manage → Subset Variables**, and select all of the variables in the table. Type "exam1_copy" (without quotes) in the *New Table Name text field*, and press the *OK button*. You will now have a copy of exam1. A benefit of using this method to copy a table is that all of the item scoring information is copied to the new table too.

Notes

1 This option is not recommend because the white space functions differently for text variables than it does for numeric variables. A white space is treated as a legitimate text value, but not a legitimate numeric value. Therefore, the white space is only converted to a null value for numeric variables.
2 Because white spaces can be problematic, you should remove them before doing an import. Open the delimited file in a plain text editor such as Notepad. Do a search for a comma followed by a white space (i.e. ", "), and replace it with nothing.

2

ITEM SCORING

A database table in jMetrik may contain a variety of data types, such as demographic variables and test items. All variables are initially treated as either text or numbers and are listed as a "Not Item" on the *Variables tab*. jMetrik has no way to know which variables may be test items and which ones may be some other type of data. You must provide additional information for jMetrik to distinguish between test items and variables that are not items. Item scoring is the process of identifying test items in the database and providing scores for each possible response option. Item scoring does not change the data table. Rather, it stores scoring information in a separate table and converts item responses to score values during an analysis. This functionality allows you to change the answer key at any time.

jMetrik offers three different item scoring methods. Two of them involve the graphical user interface (GUI), and one involves direct processing of a jMetrik command. The two GUI methods actually just build the jMetrik scoring command and process it behind the scenes. This approach is the easiest to use, and it displays the corresponding command in the jMetrik log.

Item scoring information is stored in the database as a text value referred to as the score string. You can view the score string for each item in the scoring column of the *Variables tab* in jMetrik. You never write or edit the score string directly. Rather, jMetrik creates it from the information you provide through the GUI or scoring command. The score string is described in detail to help you understand the way jMetrik works and the structure of the scoring command.

The score string consists of a list of response option codes and a list of numeric score values. Each list is comma delimited and enclosed in parentheses. Position is important in each list. The first element in the option list is assigned the score value of the first element in the score list. Likewise, the second element in the option list is assigned the value of the second element in the score list. As an example, suppose that a test item has four response options—A, B, C, and D— and option B is the correct answer. The score string is (A,B,C,D)(0,1,0,0). It tells jMetrik that option A is scored as 0 points, option B is scored as 1 point, option C is scored as 0 points, and option D is scored as 0 points. Because this item has only two score levels (i.e. 0 and 1), it is considered to be a binary item. After scoring for this item is processed, the *Variables tab* in jMetrik will show this variable type to be a "Binary Item."

The score string is flexible, and it can indicate multiple correct answers. Suppose that both option B and option D are correct answers. The score string would be (A,B,C,D)(0,1,0,1). Notice that a score of 1 point is assigned to options B and D.

Psychological measures often use Likert items where the response options are, for example, "Strongly Disagree," "Disagree," "Agree," and "Strongly Agree." There is no wrong answer for these types of items, and a score value is assigned to every category. If the item has more than two score levels, it is referred to as a polytomous item. Educational measures also make use of polytomous items when partial credit is assigned to a test item. For example, suppose a test requires examinees to write an essay and that raters score each essay from 0 to 5 points with a score of 0 representing no credit and a score of 5 representing full credit. Scores of 1, 2, 3, and 4 all represent different levels of partial credit. jMetrik distinguishes between binary and polytomous items because each may require different statistical procedures. After scoring for a polytomous item is processed, the *Variables tab* in jMetrik will show this variable type to be a "Polytomous Item."

A test with Likert items would list the complete response options (e.g. Strongly Agree) on the test form itself, but the data may contain a shortened text or a numeric code to indicate the response option. For example, the data may use the codes "SD", "D", "A", and "SA" or the codes "1", "2", "3", and "4" to indicate "Strongly Disagree," "Disagree," "Agree," and "Strongly Agree," respectively. Item scoring requires that you provide the code and numeric score for each category. For example, the score string may be (SD, D, A, SA)(1,2,3,4) to indicate that the code "SD" is scored as 1 point, the code "D" is scored as 2 points, and so on. If numeric codes had been used, the score string would be (1,2,3,4)(1,2,3,4). Note that scoring must be provided even if the data contain numeric codes. It is only through the item scoring that jMetrik will know which variables are test items and which ones are not.

Polytomous items are often reverse scored. The score string easily accommodates reverse-scored items. For example, suppose the response options from the previous paragraph are reverse scored. The score string would be (SD, D, A, SA) (4,3,2,1), or if the data involve numeric codes, it would be (1,2,3,4)(4,3,2,1).

You may find that despite your best efforts at creating a good test item, some categories are rarely selected by examinees. To avoid low counts, you may find it helpful to collapse categories. You can collapse categories in the score string by assigning the same score to multiple response options. For example, suppose the options "SD" and "D" are collapsed together and the scores "A" and "SA" are collapsed. The score string would be (SD,D,A,SA)(0,0,1,1), and it has the effect of converting a polytomous item into a binary item.

You will never write the score string yourself. jMetrik provides two methods for creating a score string in a more user friendly way. Basic item scoring allows you to edit scoring for an entire test, and it is a quick way to complete item scoring. It has a few limitations, but you will find it suitable for most purposes. Advanced item scoring provides finer control over item scoring. It also provides functionality that is not available in basic item scoring.

Omitted and Not Reached Codes

Testing often involves two special types of missing data: omitted and not reached. An omitted response is missing data that occurs when an examinee answers one or more questions before the omitted value and one or more questions after the omitted value. It is often assumed that an omitted response occurs because the examinee did not know the correct answer and so chooses to skip the question. Consequently, omitted responses are typically scored as 0 points in operational scoring (e.g. when producing test scores).

A not reached response happens when an examinee answers one or more questions before the excluded response and none of the questions after it. The conventional assumption is that a not reached response occurs because an examinee ran out of time before reaching the question. That is, the examinee had no opportunity to answer the question. As such, not reached responses are ignored in operational scoring, and an examinee's score is only based on the completed and omitted questions.

jMetrik allows you to specify your own codes for omitted and not reached responses. You must use codes that match the type of data for the variable. If examinee responses are recorded in the data as letters (e.g. A, B, C), then your omitted and not reached codes must also be one or more letters (e.g. O, N) with no spaces or punctuation between them. On the other hand, if examinee responses are recorded in the data as numbers (e.g. 1, 2, 3, 4), then your omitted and not reached codes must be numeric (e.g. −8, −9).

There are two important notes to consider when using codes for omitted and not reached responses. First, only use these codes for variables that represent test questions. If you use them for variables that are not items, they will be treated as valid data and included in the calculations when they should actually be excluded from the calculations. Second, the type of code (letter or number) must match the type of data in a variable (letters or numbers). jMetrik will display an error message if you run an analysis with missing data, omitted, and not reached codes that do not match the type of data in the data set.

Depending on the type of analysis, jMetrik allows you to handle missing, omitted, and not reached responses differently. You may choose to treat all of them as missing and ignore them during an analysis. Or, you may score the missing and omitted responses as 0 points while ignoring the not reached responses. Your choices for handling missing, omitted, and not reached responses will differ according to the options available for the method of analysis you are using. More information about these options is available in subsequent chapters that describe details for each type of analysis. However, omitted and not reached codes are not fully implemented in version 3. Complete functionality for omitted and not reached codes will be added in later versions of the software.

In the following comma delimited data listing, the omitted code is "O", and the not reached code is "N". The following data are for a test in which the first four examinees were given questions V3, V4, V5, and V6 and the last four examinees were given questions V1, V2, V3, and V4. This is the type of configuration that would be observed when two groups of examinees take two different test forms that share a common set of items (V3 and V4). The white space is present to indicate test questions that were never presented to the examinees.[1] As such, missing data has a different meaning than omitted and not reached responses. See, for example, the entry for EX5. That examinee did not reach V3 and V4, and the last two items were never presented. Finally, notice that EX3 omitted a response to V4, and EX6 omitted a response to V3 as indicated by the letter "O".

```
ID,V1,V2,V3,V4,V5,V6
EX1,  ,  ,A,B,A,C
EX2,  ,  ,B,C,A,C
EX3,  ,  ,D,O,A,B
EX4,  ,  ,C,C,B,C
EX5,A,B,N,N,  ,
EX6,A,B,O,D,  ,
EX7,A,B,D,A,  ,
EX8,A,C,D,A,  ,
```

The way you tell jMetrik about your special codes depends on the scoring procedure that you follow. Basic item scoring allows only a single code for omitted responses and a single code for not reached responses. Advanced item scoring is more flexible, and it allows each item to have its own omitted code and its own not reached code.

Basic Item Scoring

After importing a data file into jMetrik, you can apply item scoring to it. You can use either basic item scoring or advanced item scoring. Each method has its advantages and limitations. Basic item scoring allows users to easily provide an answer key for a table in jMetrik. It allows for both binary and polytomous scored items. There are two pieces of information that you must provide for basic item scoring: an answer key and the number of response options. You may use numbers (0–9) or letters (A–Z, a–z) for the answer key, but the same type of values must be found in the data. Moreover, if you use letters for the key, the case of the answer key must match the case of the data.

Multiple-Choice Items

An example excerpt from the *Basic Item Scoring dialog* for a multiple-choice test is listed below. To view this dialog in jMetrik, click **Transform → Basic Item Scoring**. Type the answer key in the first row of the table in the dialog, and type the number of response options in the second row.

Figure 2.1 indicates that item1 has A for a correct answer, and there are four response options. Since the key is the letter A, jMetrik assumes the four response options are ordered letters starting with A (i.e. A, B, C, D). As a second example, the correct answer for item2 is C, and the four response options are A, B, C, and D.

You may also use numbers for the correct answer provided that the responses are numbers in the data file. If you use numbers, basic item scoring will assume they are all positive integers between 1 and the number of response options (inclusive). For example, the previous example could be rewritten as shown in Figure 2.2, if the data are coded as numbers instead of letters.

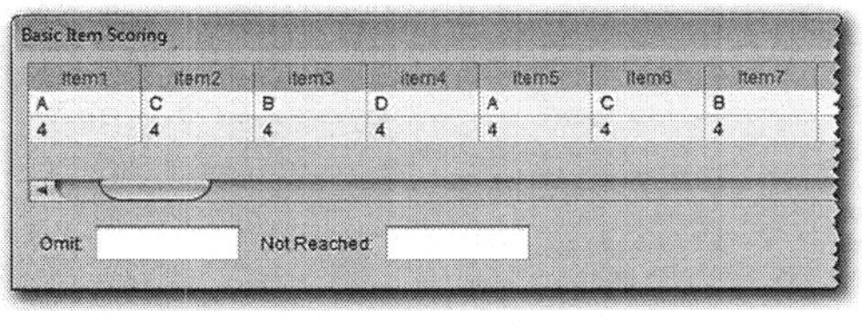

FIGURE 2.1 Basic item scoring with letters

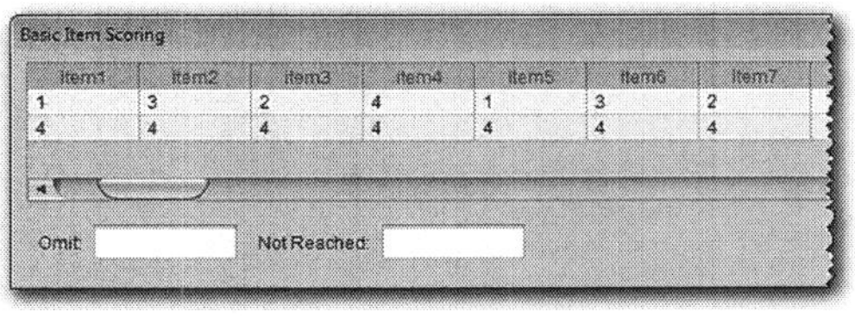

FIGURE 2.2 Basic item scoring with numbers

If your data file contains letters and numbers, use both in the answer key. For example, suppose that the first four items of a multiple choice test have data that are letters and the latter three have data that are numbers (see Figure 2.3). The correct answers for the first two items are A and C, and the correct answers for the fifth and sixth items are 1 and 3. All items have four response options. Basic item scoring assumes the items coded as letters have A, B, C, and D as the response options and the items coded as numbers have 1, 2, 3, and 4 as the response options.

Note that even though numbers are used in the data for this example, the items are all binary scored items. The number in the answer key indicates the correct answer, not the number of points awarded for a response.

Polytomous Items

Polytomous items do not have a single correct answer. As such, the answer key for a polytomous item should be a + or a − sign followed by a number to indicate where the scoring begins. The + sign tells jMetrik to count forward by the number of response options. The − sign tells jMetrik to count backwards. For example, suppose item4, item5, item6, and item7 are polytomous items scored as shown in Figure 2.4.

Item4 is a polytomous item with four categories scored in ascending order starting at 1 (i.e. 1, 2, 3, 4). Item5 is also a four-category polytomous item, but the scoring starts at 0 as indicated by the +0 (i.e. 0, 1, 2, 3). Item6 and item7 are reverse-scored items. Scoring for item6 begins at 4 and counts backwards for four increments (i.e. 4, 3, 2, 1). Scoring for item7 starts at 3 as indicated by the −3 and

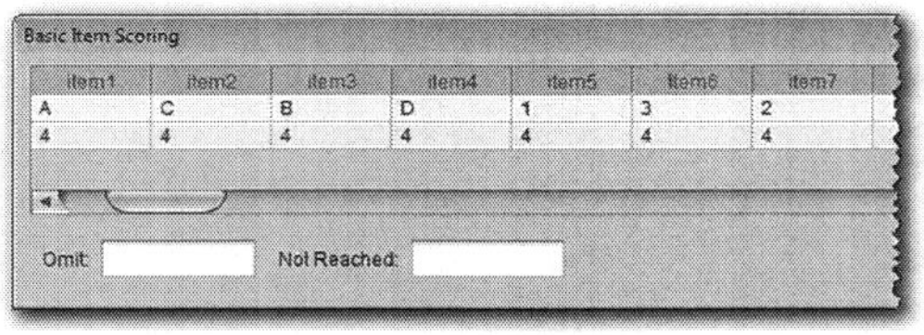

FIGURE 2.3 Basic item scoring with letters and numbers

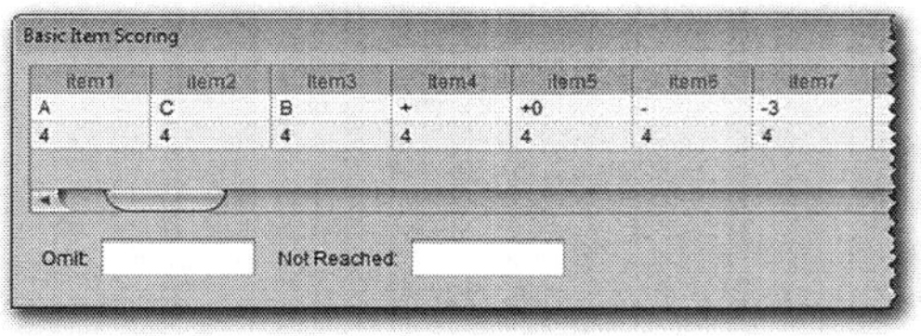

FIGURE 2.4 Basic item scoring with binary and polytomous items

counts backwards for four increments (i.e. 3, 2, 1, 0). These four examples show various ways polytomous items can be quickly scored in the *Basic Item Scoring dialog.*

Not Items

To tell jMetrik that a variable is not an item, do not provide a value for the answer key or number of response options. You can remove scoring for an item in the same way. If you would like to clear the scoring information and convert an item to a "Not Item," then delete the answer key entry and value for the number of response options.

Handling Errors in Basic Item Scoring

It is possible for users to input the wrong information in basic item scoring. Four possible errors are handled automatically in the following ways. The lowest possible value for a polytomous item is 0. If you specify too many response categories for a reverse-scored polytomous item, negative scores will not be used. Scores of 0 will be assigned to items where the counting would be negative. For example, it you have two items scored as shown in Figure 2.5, the scoring for item6 will be 3, 2, 1, 0, 0, and the scoring for item7 will be 3, 2, 1, 0, 0, 0.

A second possible error occurs when a user does not provide an answer key or does not provide the number of response options. In each case, jMetrik will not score the item, and the variable will become a "Not Item." For example, the scoring shown in Figure 2.6 will cause jMetrik to treat item6 and item7 as a

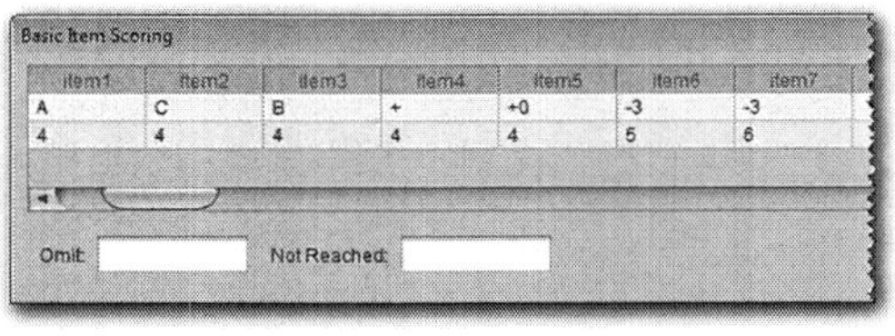

FIGURE 2.5 Basic item scoring with alternate polytomous scoring

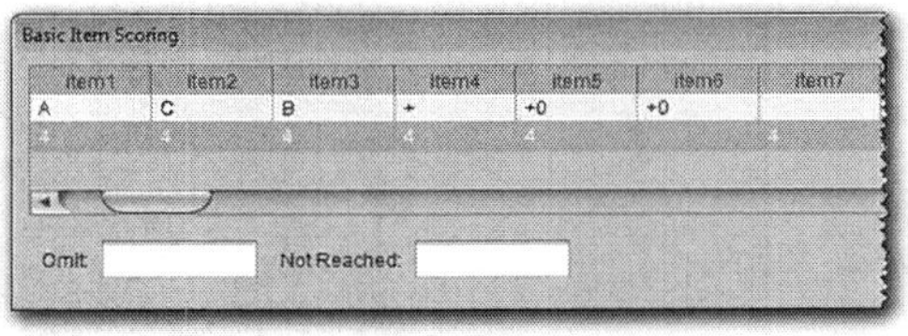

FIGURE 2.6 Converting removing item scoring

FIGURE 2.7 Basic item scoring with incorrect input

"Not Item." Scoring will only be accepted for variables that have both a key and number of response options.

Finally, a user may provide an answer key that exceeds the number of response options. In this situation, jMetrik uses the larger value. The scoring shown in Figure 2.7 will be automatically adjusted for item4 because the answer key "D" is larger than the number of response options "3". Scoring will be automatically adjusted such that the number of response options is 4.

The main limitation of basic item scoring is that you can only indicate one correct answer for each item. If you need to indicate multiple correct answers for an item, then you must use the advanced item scoring tool. A second limitation is that categories may not be collapsed using basic item scoring. You must you advanced item scoring to combine multiple response categories.

Advanced Item Scoring

Advanced item scoring is similar to the scoring method in earlier versions of jMetrik. It gives you fine control over the scoring of individual items and response options. Advanced item scoring allows you to provide multiple correct answers for an item, combine response categories, and use different omitted and not reached codes for individual items. You can score individual items or all of your items with advanced item scoring. Advanced item scoring is also the ideal way to reuse an answer key. If you have multiple data files that use the same answer key and have the same item names, use advanced item scoring and save the syntax from the log file. You can reuse the advanced scoring command with other tables in the database. The steps to using advanced item scoring are (a) open the dialog, (b) provide the response options and option scores, (c) select items, (d) submit item scoring, (e) repeat steps b through d as needed, and (f) press the *OK button* to process the command. Details of these steps are described in the next few paragraphs.

Start the *Advanced Item Scoring dialog* by clicking **Transform** → **Advanced Item Scoring**. A dialog like the one shown in Figure 2.8 will appear and allow you to score each item.

Each row of the *Option/Score table* must contain the response option code in the option column and the corresponding score for the response option in the

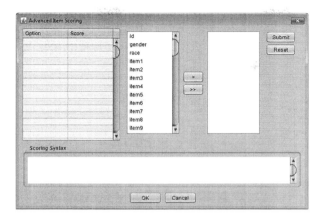

FIGURE 2.8 Advanced Item Scoring dialog

score column. For example, if the code "A" (without quotes) is the correct answer, type it in the first column of the *Option/Score table*, and then type "1" (without quotes) in the score column of the same row. This information tells jMetrik that 1 point is awarded for a response of "A". Suppose now that option "B" is incorrect. Type "B" (without quotes) in the option column of the next row, and type "0" in the score column of the same row. This information tells jMetrik that a response of "B" is awarded 0 points. Continue with the remaining response options in a similar fashion. Once you have provided all of the options and scores, you then select the items for which the scoring applies.

It is common for multiple items to share the same item scoring (e.g. multiple items with "A" as the correct response). In the *Item selection panel*, you can select all of the items that will use the scoring provided in the option score table. Click an item and press the *Select button* to move it to the *Selected item list*. To select multiple items at once, hold down the control button (command button on a Mac) while clicking each item. Then press the *Select button* to move the items to the *Selected item list*.

Once your selections are complete, press the *Submit button*. This action will produce scoring syntax and display it in the *Scoring Syntax area*. You can then provide scoring for another set of items. Items for which you have already provided scoring will appear in bold font in the *Unselected item list*. This behavior is to help you keep track of the scoring you have already completed. However, if you provide new scoring for an item already selected, jMetrik will use whatever scoring is processed last. Provide the scoring, select items, and press the *Submit button* for each group of items (or individual items) you are scoring.

After you have completed this process for all of the items you would like to score, press the *OK button* to execute the scoring command and process the scoring. The dialog will close once you press the *OK button.* If you would like to close the dialog without processing the scoring, press the *Cancel button.*

Advanced item scoring allows you to have different omitted and not reached codes for each item. For an omit code, type the omit code in the option column of the *Option/Score table,* and type the value "OM" (upper case and without quotes) in the corresponding score column. "OM" is a reserved value that tells jMetrik that an option is actually an omit code. You cannot use the value "OM" as a response option in your data table. Not reached items are handled similarly. Type the not reached code in the option column and the value "NR" (without quotes) in the score column. "NR" is also a reserved value and cannot be used as a response option in your data table. As noted earlier, omitted and not reached codes are not fully implemented in version 3.

Figure 2.9 shows and example of advanced item scoring. In this figure, option A is scored as 1 point, and options B, C, and D are scored as 0 points. The option O is specified as the omit code, and the option N is specified as the not reached code. Note that special codes are provided in this example, but they are not required in advanced item scoring. If you do not have omitted and not reached codes in your data, there is no need to use the special codes "OM" and "NR." Item1, item5, and item6 are selected in Figure 2.9. Scoring syntax for these items will be generated (but not processed) once the *Submit button* is pressed. The command will appear in the *Scoring Syntax area* as options = (A,B,C,D), scores = (1,0,0,0), omit = O, nr = N, variables = (item1, item5, item6);.

Advanced item scoring takes more time to complete, but it provides greater flexibility in scoring individual items. Basic item scoring will be adequate and faster most of the time, but you must use advanced item scoring if you have an item with

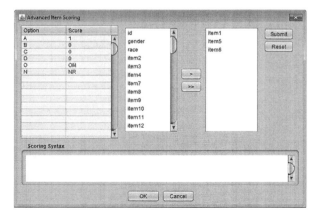

FIGURE 2.9 Advanced Item Scoring dialog example with special codes

multiple correct answers or if you need to combine or collapse categories. Figure 2.10 shows an example of an item with multiple correct answers. Notice that for `item7` a score of 1 is provided for options A and C. Both of these options are correct answers.

Likert scale items with many categories may have some categories that are selected by few or even no examinees. In such a case, you might want to combine an empty or sparse category with another one that is selected more frequently. An example of combining multiple categories is shown in Figure 2.11. `Item12` is a Likert scale item with response options 0 through 6. However, very few people selected categories 5 and 6. Therefore, these categories are combined with category 4 by assigning a score of 4 to options 4, 5, and 6.

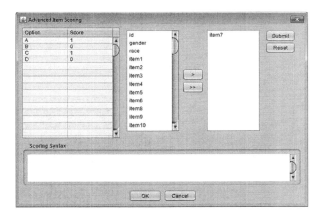

FIGURE 2.10 Multiple correct answers and advanced item scoring

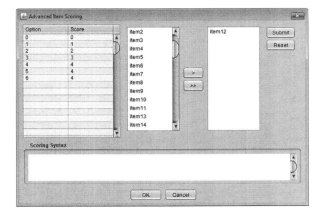

FIGURE 2.11 Collapsing categories with advanced item scoring

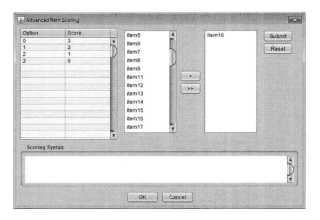

FIGURE 2.12 Reverse scoring example

Likert scale items are often worded in the opposite direction from the response options (e.g. low scores are stronger indicators of the construct). In this situation, you will likely want to reverse score the items so that large values always indicate a greater presence of the construct. You can also reverse score polytomous items through the advanced item scoring dialog. Figure 2.12 demonstrates the way option values of 0, 1, 2, and 3 are reverse scored as 3, 2, 1, 0 for item10. You can reverse score a single item or multiple items in this way.

Not Items

To remove scoring for an item and convert it to a "Not Item," start the *Advanced Item Scoring dialog* and select the item. Do not provide any scoring information for the item. Leave the *Option/Score table* blank. Press the *Submit button* and then the *OK button* to process the scoring information. This will remove any scoring that has been set for the selected item. For example, suppose you accidentally provided scoring information for the race variable. Follow the steps for converting this variable to a "Not Item." When you press the *Submit button*, the syntax will appear as options = (), scores = (), variables = (race); . Notice that the options and scores arguments are equal to an empty set (i.e. nothing is listed in parentheses). This syntax tells jMetrik to remove the item scoring for the variable race.

Scoring with the jMetrik Commands

jMetrik provides three ways to provide item scoring and convert variables into items. Two methods allow you to provide the scoring information via the interface, and the third option allows you to use the scoring commands. The dialog methods are convenient, and each one has its strengths and limitations. Basic item scoring is fast but provides limited capabilities. Advanced item scoring takes more time but gives you greater control over item scoring. Advanced item scoring is also ideal for reusing the scoring command on other tables that have the same answer key. Finally, both basic and advanced item scoring have a command that is run in the background. You can edit and process these commands directly if you prefer to work with syntax instead of dialogs.

The *Basic Item Scoring dialog* and *Advanced Item Scoring dialog* are tools for building scoring commands. To see the commands after you complete either of the dialogs, open the log file. Basic item scoring is done with the `bscoring` command, and advanced item scoring uses the `scoring` command. The advanced item scoring command is the preferred way to conduct scoring with a command and apply the same `scoring` command to multiple data tables. You can copy the scoring command from the log file and save it in a new text file so that you can reuse the syntax with another data table. Saving the command is useful if you have multiple tables in the database that use the same scoring. As long as the item names are the same, you can reuse the advanced scoring command on another table. The only necessary change to the command is that the table name must reflect the target data table.

To reuse a scoring command, the item names in the command must match the item names in the table to be scored. Paste the scoring command into a new text file in jMetrik, or open it as a text file in the program. The only line you must edit in the command is the data line [e.g. `data (db = mydb, table = EXAM1);`]. Change `table = EXAM1` to `table = READING` if you want to apply the scoring to a table called reading. Execute the command by clicking **Commands → Run Command**. After the command has been processed, the new scoring will be visible in the *Variables tab*.

Note

1 As stated earlier, a white space is not a recommended method for indicating missing data. White spaces are used in this example to keep the columns properly aligned for better readability.

3

TEST SCALING

Test scaling is the process of converting test performances into meaningful numbers. It begins with scoring individual items and combining them into a raw score such as the sum score or percent correct score. Raw scores convey adequate information for classroom teachers and researchers, particularly when they represent performance on a one-off test. They are less adequate for standardized testing programs that use multiple versions of a test and produce scores over a number of years. Standardized tests typically involve a raw score transformation (i.e. a scale score) that allows for scale maintenance and consistency in score interpretation over the lifetime of the testing program. Raw scores and scale scores obtain meaning by comparing them to a frame of reference such as the performance of other examinees or a content domain represented by the test (Tong & Kolen, 2010).

Scores produced from test scaling are reported to examinees and other stakeholders who make decisions according to the results. For example, a psychologist may decide to initiate services for a child with low scores on an intelligence test or a teacher may promote a student that meets proficiency standards on a course exam. Therefore, test scaling is usually conducted at the end of the test development process and only involves test questions that pass quality control procedures (e.g. item analysis, DIF analysis). This chapter is presented before those that discuss quality control procedures because jMetrik often requires you to create a preliminary test score during an analysis. Once the quality control procedures are complete, you must repeat the test scaling process and produce a final set of test scores that you report to examinees and other stakeholders.

Raw Scores

Kolen (2006) describes two types of scores in test scaling: raw scores and scale scores. Raw scores are transformations of item scores. The most common example is the sum score, which is the sum of the number of points awarded for each test item. The sum score is so common in testing that the terms raw score and sum score are often used interchangeably. However, there are other transformations of the item scores including the average score, percent correct score, and Kelley's regressed score.

The average score is simply the total number of points awarded for each test item divided by the total number of points possible on the test. If all test questions are binary items (i.e. scored right or wrong), then the average score can be multiplied by 100 to produce the percent correct score. The percent correct score is also referred to as a domain score, particularly in the context of criterion-referenced testing, as it is an estimate of the percentage of items in the domain that an examinee can answer correctly.

Sum scores and percent correct scores are estimates of an examinee's true score, but they are affected by measurement error (see chapter 5). Kelley's regressed score is a better estimate of the true score because it accounts for measurement error. Kelley's regressed score involves an examinee's raw score, X; the average raw score for the group, $\bar{X}$; and an estimate of score reliability, $\hat{\rho}_{XX'}$. It is given by $E(\tau|X) = X(\hat{\rho}_{XX'}) + \bar{X}(1 - \hat{\rho}_{XX'})$. If there is no measurement error, reliability equals 1 and the true score estimate is the same as the raw score. On the other hand, if reliability is 0, then Kelley's estimate of the true score is the group mean. Kelley's regressed score is a biased but less variable estimate of the true score than the raw score (Kolen, 2006).

Scale Scores

Raw scores are easy to compute, but the raw score scale is vulnerable to test modifications that affect test difficulty and the distribution of scores. The raw score scale may change whenever you add, remove, or replace items on a test. For example, a test composed of 10 binary items has a raw score scale that ranges from 0 to 10, but adding 2 items to the test changes the scale to range from 0 to 12. There is no way to compare scores from the 12-item test to those from the 10-item test without making any adjustments to the scale. Even if the number of items remains the same, replacing difficult items with easier ones will affect the score distribution. Examinees will appear to earn higher scores while in reality the test is easier. Multiple versions of the same test also involve differences in test difficulty and scores that are not directly comparable. Although differences in test difficulty and the distribution of scores may be overcome with test equating, the consistency of score interpretation is achieved through the use of a common score scale and the conversion of raw scores to scale scores.

A scale score is a transformation of a raw score that facilitates score interpretation. Linear transformations have the form $X^\star = AX + B$, where X is a raw score and A and B are the slope and intercept coefficient, respectively. Kolen (2006) describes two ways of computing these coefficients. The first way involves a score scale defined by its mean, μ, and standard deviation, σ. Using the raw score mean, $\bar{X}$, and standard deviation, S, the coefficients are $A = \sigma/S$ and $B = \mu - A\bar{X}$. A linear transformation involving these coefficients will result in scale scores that have the desired mean and standard deviation, but there is no restriction on the minimum and maximum possible values. Scale scores could take on numbers outside a desired range of scores; they could take on negative values when only positive scores are desired. Constraints may be applied to keep scores in a desired range (i.e. truncation), such as changing negative numbers to 0. However, these constraints can affect the linear nature of the transformation (Kolen, 2006).

The second way to find the slope and intercept involves two score points, such as the minimum and maximum values. Let λ_{max} be the maximum possible scale score and λ_{min} be the minimum possible scale score. Similarly, let X_{max} and X_{min} be the maximum and minimum possible raw score values, respectively. The slope is then $A = (\lambda_{max} - \lambda_{min})/(X_{max} - X_{min})$, and the intercept is $B = \lambda_{min} - AX_{min}$. This way of computing coefficients leads to scale scores that are within the desired range, but there is no restriction on the mean or standard deviation.

Although there are two ways to create a linear transformation, you do not need both of them. Choose the method that is aligned with the target score scale. If you aim to have a score scale with a specific mean and standard deviation, use the first method. If you would like to have a score scale with a particular minimum and maximum value and you are not concerned about the mean and standard deviation, then use the second approach.

Nonlinear transformations in test scaling include any monotonic nondecreasing function. This type of function preserves the ordering of scores but not necessarily the intervals between them. Percentile ranks and normalized scores are two examples of nonlinear transformations in testing applications. To compute percentile ranks, let $F(x)$ be the discrete cumulative distribution function of the observed scores, which indicates the proportion of examinees scoring at or below x. Now let M be the maximum possible test score and $x^\star$ be the smallest integer closest to $x + 0.5$. The percentile rank, $P(x)$ is computed in the following way (Kolen & Brennan, 2004):

$$P(x) = 100\{F(x^\star - 1) + [x - (x^\star - 0.5)][F(x^\star) - F(x^\star - 1)]\},$$
$$-0.5 \le x < M + 0.5$$
$$= 0, \qquad x < -0.5$$
$$= 100, \qquad x \ge M + 0.5.$$

Percentile ranks range between 0 and 100 and indicate the proportion of examinees scoring at or below a particular score. For example, a score with a percentile rank of 85 indicates that 85% of examinees earned a score at or below the same level. Similarly, 30% of examinees earn a score at or below a percentile rank of 30. Note that percentile ranks are not suitable scores for all testing applications. You need a sample size of several thousand examinees to obtain stable percentile ranks.

You can use percentile ranks as scores in and of themselves, or you can convert them to percentiles from a probability distribution. Normalized scores are percentile scores from the normal distribution. The normalized score conversion is expressed as $z = \Phi^{-1}[P(x)]$ where Φ^{-1} indicates the inverse standard normal cumulative distribution function (Crocker & Algina, 1986) and $P(x)$ is the percentile rank of the raw score x. For example, a percentile rank of 10 corresponds to a normalized score of $z = \Phi^{-1}(.10) = -1.282$, and a percentile rank of 95 corresponds to a normalized score of $z = \Phi^{-1}(.95) = 1.645$. You can linearly transform values from the standard normal distribution to any normal distribution with a mean, μ, and a standard deviation of σ, using $z^\star = z\sigma + \mu$. For example, T-scores use $\mu = 50$ and $\sigma = 10$, and Wechsler IQ scores have a scale with $\mu = 100$ and $\sigma = 15$. Continuing with the previous example, a percentile rank of 10 corresponds to a T-score of 37.18 and a percentile rank of 95 corresponds to a T-score of 66.45. In practice, these scores would be rounded to integers resulting in T-scores of 37 and 66, respectively.

Normal scores are another way to produce scores from a normal distribution. Normal scores are computed from the raw score ranks instead of the percentile ranks. For example, van der Waerden's normal score is given by $z_{vw} = \Phi^{-1}[r/(n + 1)]$, where r is the rank of a raw score and n is the total number of examinees. There are two other types of normal scores. Tukey's normal score is $z_T = \Phi^{-1}[(r - 1/3)/(n + 1/3)]$, and Blom's normal score is $z_B = \Phi^{-1}[(r - 3/8)/(n + 1/4)]$. Normal scores are commonly encountered in nonparametric statistics such as nonparametric item response theory. You would rarely use them as test scores in an operational testing program. You are more likely to use normal scores during an analysis while evaluating items for quality assurance.

Note that converting raw scores to normalized scores or normal scores forces the data to be normally distributed (i.e. bell shaped). If the raw score distribution is symmetric and unimodal, then this conversion is a good approximation. On the other hand, if the raw score distribution is substantially skewed, then normalized scores or normal scores are only a rough approximation of the raw score distribution.

Frame of Reference

Meaning is added to raw scores and scale scores by comparing them to a frame of reference such as the performance of other examinees or a content domain.

A norm is the distribution of scores for a representative sample of examinees from the target population. It is characterized by statistics such as the mean, standard deviation, and percentile ranks (Kolen, 2006). Norm-referenced scores such as percentile ranks and normalized scores allow for relative comparisons among examinees and permit statements such as "Jill scored above average" or "Trevor performed better than 86% of examinees." It is through the norm (i.e. the performance of others) that a score takes on meaning. However, the interpretation of a norm-referenced score is not absolute. It is relative to the target population. Norms can be created for different populations. A national norm represents the distribution of scores from a nationally representative sample of examines, and a local norm may be the distribution of student scores within a school district. Because the interpretation is relative, a low score on a national norm may be a high score on a local norm. If you change the norm, you also change the interpretation of scores.

The Wechsler Intelligence Scale for Children—Fourth Edition (WISC-IV) is an example of a norm-referenced test. The WISC-IV is an intelligence test that aims to compare the neurocognitive and information processing capabilities of a child to a nationally representative group of similar-age children (Williams, Weiss, & Rolfhus, 2003). National norms describe the distribution of scores for WISC-IV examinees in a particular age group. Because this test is norm-referenced, psychologists can use it to identify exceptionally high scoring examinees such intellectually gifted children and distinguish between unusually low scoring examinees with mild or moderate mental retardation. College entrance exams are another example of a norm-referenced test. A college admissions office may only be able to accept a small portion of applicants for the incoming class. Consequently, the admissions office may decide to accept only the highest scoring applicants.

Not all tests involve relative comparisons among examinees. In a criterion-referenced test, the frame of reference is a content domain, and examinee scores reflect the degree of achievement in the domain. Score interpretation hinges on the clear definition of the content domain and the alignment of the test to the domain. This work usually falls to subject matter experts such as math educators or English language arts teachers that provide information about what students at different grade levels should know and be able to do. Subject matter experts also review tests to check their alignment with a domain. Score interpretation fails if either the content domain is poorly specified or the test lacks alignment. A well-specified domain and properly aligned test permits statements such as "Mateo answered 92% of the items correctly" and "He passed the test." That is, criterion-referenced scores may be expressed as the percentage of items answered correctly or as a statement about the student's achievement level (e.g. fail, pass, or high pass). Percentage correct scores can be computed directly from examinee responses, but achievement level scores require the use of a standard setting process to establish the cut scores that demark the boundaries between achievement levels (see Cizek & Bunch, 2007). Standard setting also involves expert judgment about test content and the knowledge and skills of students at each achievement level.

The Virginia Standards of Learning Assessments are examples of a criterion-referenced test (Virginia Department of Education, 2012). The Standards of Learning (SOLs) define academic content in reading, writing, math, science, and history. They are expounded upon in a set of curriculum frameworks that further define the content measured by the assessments and provide guidance to teachers implementing the state curriculum in their classrooms. Test blueprints guide test development and indicate the proportion of each content area measured by the test. Blueprints also provide information about the item types and supplemental materials students can use during testing (e.g. calculators). Experts and stakeholders participated in all aspects of test development starting with the specification of the SOLs and continuing through test design. These groups included classroom teachers, curriculum specialists, business leaders, and other Virginia educators. Students receive a scale score describing their performance on the test as well as an achievement level score (e.g. Fail/Below Basic, Fail/Basic, Pass/Proficient, and Pass/Advanced). These scores are interpreted in the context of the SOL content domain. Licensure and certification exams are other examples of criterion-referenced tests. These tests help protect the public by ensuring that examinees who pass the tests demonstrate a level of competency that is minimally acceptable for practice.

Although many tests can be classified as either norm or criterion referenced, it is not uncommon to find a test with both frames of reference. Educational tests often report a pass/fail score along with a percentile rank. The goal is to not only identify students who have mastered the tested content but also make finer distinctions among examinees in terms of their performance. Some types of scores are suitable for norm-referenced tests, whereas others are appropriate for criterion-referenced tests. As indicated in the previous example, the pass/fail categorization of an examinee's performance is a criterion-referenced score, but a percentile rank of, say, 82 is a norm-referenced score. Whenever a test involves multiple score interpretations, you should report a score for each one. This practice will help ensure that test users have score information that is aligned with the type of decision at hand.

Note that a frame of reference is established through test design and data collection. Test scaling will make the connection between the frame of reference and test scores, but it will not create the frame of reference. There is no analysis you can conduct in jMetrik that will produce the frames of reference. You must collect data from a representative sample from the population in a norm-referenced test, and you must have a well-defined content domain for a criterion-referenced test.

Running the Analysis in jMetrik

jMetrik provides three different menu options related to test scaling. All three are located in the *Transform menu*. The *Test Scaling menu item* produces a dialog that contains options for creating raw scores and linear and nonlinear transformations of the raw score. To run the test scaling analysis, click **Transform → Test Scaling** to display the dialog (see Figure 3.1). You will see the *Variable Selection panel* at the top of the dialog. Any variable you select will be included in the computation of the score.

Test Scaling Options

The *Score panel* includes a text field where you can type a name for the score variable that is created and added to the table at the completion of the analysis. A drop-down menu in the *Score panel* allows you to select the type of score you would like to produce. The raw score options include the *Sum score*, *Average score*, and *Kelley score*. jMetrik uses Guttman's lambda-2 as the reliability estimate (see chapter 5) in the computation of Kelley's regressed score. Nonlinear transformation options in the *Score panel* include *Percentile rank* and *Normalized score*. These are both computed from the sum score.

The *Linear Transformation panel* allows you to specify values for the linear transformation that is applied to raw scores and normalized scores. The *Linear Transformation panel* contains two text fields. The one labeled *Mean* is where you type the

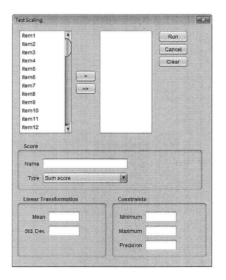

FIGURE 3.1 Test Scaling dialog

desired mean, μ, for the scale, and the one labeled *Std. Dev.* is where you provide the desired standard deviation of the scale, σ. The linear transformation step is optional. Leave the text fields blank if you choose not to transform your scores. Note also that linear transformations are not applied to percentile ranks.

A linear transformation can lead to scores that have decimal values and exceed a range of scores. The *Constraints panel* allows you to truncate and round scores to avoid out-of-range scores and noninteger values. To produce scores with a desired number of decimal places (usually none), type a value in the *Precision text field* of the *Constraints panel*. For example, typing 0 will round the scores to the nearest integer, and typing 2 will round scores to the nearest hundredth. You can also provide the desired minimum and maximum score values in the corresponding text fields of the *Constraints panel*. Be sure to use minimum and maximum values that are within the desired score scale. Otherwise, you could produce scores that are the same for everyone. For example, if you specify a minimum value of 300 for your sum scores, but the sum scores only take on values between 0 and 60, then everyone will be assigned a score of 300.

After configuring the options in the *Test Scaling dialog*, press the *Run button* to execute the analysis. jMetrik will add a new variable to the data table containing the scores and produce a new tab that summarizes the results. If you produce Kelley scores, percentile ranks, or normalized scores, jMetrik will list the raw to scale score conversion table in the output.

Missing Data

In jMetrik, missing item responses are scored as incorrect when producing a sum score. This subsequently affects all other scores produced by the test scaling procedures in jMetrik (i.e. percentile ranks are based on sum scores, and normalized scores are based on percentile ranks). The one exception is the average score. The average score only involves test items completed by an examinee. It is computed as the sum of the item scores for the completed items divided by the number of completed items.

Additional jMetrik Dialogs

jMetrik provides a second option for producing a linear transformation of a numeric variable. Click **Transform → Linear Transformation** to start the *Linear Transformation dialog* (see Figure 3.2). Select the variable you would like to transform, and type a name for the new variable in the text field with the *New Variable Name label*. The last two panels in this dialog give you control over the type of linear transformation you would like to produce. As described earlier, you can compute transformation coefficients in one of two ways. You can either (a) provide the scale mean and standard deviation or (b) provide two scale

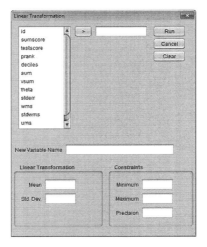

FIGURE 3.2 Linear Transformation dialog

values such as the minimum and maximum values. If you would like to create a transformation with the desired mean and standard deviation, then type the new scale mean in the text field labeled *Mean* and type the new scale standard deviation in the text field labeled *Std. Dev.* You can optionally round the results and truncate scores to minimum and maximum values by inputting information in the *Constraints panel* of this dialog.

If you would like your new scale to have a specific minimum and maximum value, then leave the *Linear Transformation text fields* blank. Do not provide a value for *Mean* and *Std. Dev.* Provide the new scale minimum and maximum values in the respective text fields of the *Constraints panel.* This information will produce the second type of linear transformation described earlier. Note that the *Linear Transformation dialog* allows you to transform any numeric variable, not just those you might use for test scaling. Regardless of the nature of the variable (e.g. a test score or some other numeric variable), the linear transformation follows the conventions described in this chapter.

The last dialog related to test scaling is the *Rank Values dialog* (see Figure 3.3). This dialog provides options for creating ranks, rank-based groups, and normal scores. To start this dialog, click **Transform → Ranking**. In the *Variable Selection panel*, choose the numeric variable for which you would like to compute the new scores. Type a name for the new variable in the *New Variable Name text field*, and then select the type of score you would like to produce. The *Score Type drop-down box* contains various options related to ranks. The *Ranks option* ranks cases according to values of the selected variable. The *Ntiles option* assigns examinees to one of *N* quantile groups. For example, if the number of groups provided for the *Ntiles*

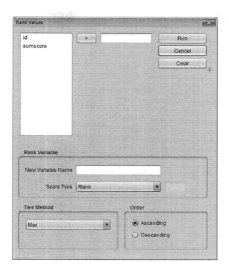

FIGURE 3.3 Rank Values dialog

option is five, then jMetrik will create five groups with each one containing 20% of the examinees. That is, the lowest 20% of scores will be in group 1, the next lowest 20% of scores will be in group 2, and so on until all examinees are placed into one of the five groups. The other options are quick options for Ntiles. The *Deciles option* is the same thing as specifying 10 groups for the Ntiles option. It will create 10 groups with each one containing 10% of examinees. Group 1 will contain the lowest 10% of scores, group 2 will contain the next lowest 10% of scores, and so on. Similarly, the *Quartiles option* is the same thing as specifying four groups for the Ntiles option.

The *Score Type drop-down menu* includes an option for *Percentile Ranks*. However, this computation of percentile ranks is different from the one in the *Test Scaling dialog*. Percentile rank computations in the *Rank Values dialog* assume the data are continuous, whereas the percentile rank computation in the *Test Scaling dialog* assumes the data are categorical. The two calculations will be similar but not exactly the same.

The remaining options in the *Score Type drop-down menu* pertain to normal scores. You can choose from Tukey, Blom, and van der Waerden normal scores in this menu. Differences in these scores were described earlier.

Ranking often involves ties that must be resolved. jMetrik provides five methods for resolving ties: maximum rank, minimum rank, sequential ranks, average rank, and random sequence ranks. By default, jMetrik assigns the maximum rank to tied values. For example, if the original values are 10, 22, 12, 22, and 30, then the ranks will be 1, 4, 2, 4, 5 when ties are assigned the maximum value. Alternatively, you can assign the minimum value to tied values, which would produce the ranks 1, 3, 2, 3, 5 for the scores in the previous example. The sequential ties option assigns ranks to tied values in the order of their appearance. This would produce the ranks 1, 3, 2, 4, 5. The average ties option is probably the most familiar. It assigns the average rank of the tied values. In this example it would yield 1, 3.5, 2, 3.5, 5. The last ties option assigns a uniform random value to each original score to break ties randomly.

The remaining two panels in the *Rank Values dialog* pertain to the way ranks are computed. By default, jMetrik ranks the cases in ascending order, but you can change this option to descending order in the *Order panel*.

Example 1: Multiple-Choice Items

In the first example, we will use the exam1 data to compute the sum score. There is already a variable called `sumscore` in the table, so we will name the new variable `testscore`. Following the steps outlined previously, we will select all of the test items to create the sum score. A new column appears in the table after the analysis is complete. If you view the data, you will notice that `sumscore` and `testscore` have identical values. That result confirms that we applied the item scoring correctly. Descriptive statistics indicate that values of `testscore` range from 1 to 56 with a mean of 30.35 and a standard deviation of 11.01. Figure 3.4 illustrates the distribution of scores in a histogram.

To compute percentile ranks, repeat the steps for starting the *Test Scaling dialog* and selecting all of the test items. Name the new variable `prank`, and select *Percentile Ranks* from the *Score Type drop-down menu*. jMetrik adds the new scores

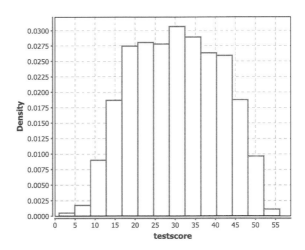

FIGURE 3.4 Histogram of exam1 sum scores

to the table and displays a sum score to percentile rank conversion table in the output. The percentile rank for the first examinee (ID = 1) is 63.38. This score indicates that examinee 1 did better than 63% of examinees taking this test. If you view percentile ranks for every examinee, you will notice that examinees with the same sum score have the same percentile rank. Therefore, the sum score to percentile rank conversion can be summarized into a table, and you do not need to view all 6,000 percentile rank scores in the data table. A portion of the score conversion table is listed in Figure 3.5. Notice that the table includes percentile ranks for sum scores that no one earned (e.g. 0 and 2 in this data set). jMetrik obtains these percentile ranks through linear interpolation.

Notice that a sum score of 10 corresponds to a percentile rank of 1.6583, and a sum score of 15 corresponds to a percentile rank of 8.5333. Thus, a difference of 5 sum score points leads to a difference of 6.875 percentile ranks at this part of the scale. If you move to another part of the scale, a difference of 5 sum score points (i.e. $30 - 25 = 5$) translates to a difference of 13.7417 percentile ranks (i.e. $48.6 - 34.8583 = 13.7417$). This result shows the nonlinear nature of the percentile rank transformation. The same difference in sum scores at two different parts of the scale leads to different differences in percentile ranks. A difference of 5 sum score points was a difference of 6.875 percentile ranks at the low end of the scale, but a difference of 5 sum score points was a difference of 13.7417 percentile ranks at a higher point on the scale. Figure 3.6 illustrates the nonlinear nature of the transformation for the entire scale.

Sum scores and percentile ranks are just two types of scores in the *Test Scaling dialog*. The next example will demonstrate the computation of normalized scores for a test composed of polytomous items. It will also demonstrate two different linear transformations. Although the examples in this chapter use tests with only binary or only polytomous items, all of the test scaling procedures in this chapter can be applied to tests composed of binary, polytomous, or mixed item types.

```
                    SCORE TABLE
         ====================================
         Original        Percentile
          Value            Rank
         ------------------------------------
             0             0.0028
             1             0.0083
             2             0.0417
             3             0.0750
             4             0.1667
             5             0.2500
             6             0.3500
             7             0.5000
             8             0.7417
             9             1.1417
            10             1.6583
            11             2.4667
            12             3.7167
            13             5.1583
            14             6.7667
            15             8.5333
            16            10.5917
            17            13.0500
            18            15.5417
            19            18.1750
            20            21.0750
            21            24.0417
```

FIGURE 3.5 Percentile rank table for exam1

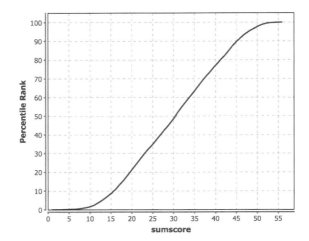

FIGURE 3.6 Line plot of percentile ranks

Example 2: Polytomous Items

Using the exam2 data, start the *Test Scaling dialog*, and select all of the test items. Type normscore as the new variable name, and choose *Normalized score* in the drop-down menu. Click the *Run button* to execute the analysis. jMetrik adds the variable normscore to the table and displays summary statistics and a score conversion table at the completion of the analysis. These scores range from −3.09 to 3.09[1] with a mean of 0 and a standard deviation of 1 because jMetrik used a standard normal distribution by default when computing normalized scores. You will rarely, if ever, report negative scores to examinees. Therefore, you should use a linear transformation to create a more useful scale. Repeat the same analysis, but this time, type tscore for the new variable name, and type 50 for the mean and 10 for the standard deviation in the *Linear Transformation panel*. Also, type a 0 in the *Precision text field* of the *Constraints panel* in order to round scores to the nearest integer. Click the *Run button* to execute the analysis. The T-scores you produced range from 19 to 81 with a mean of 49.94 and a standard deviation of 10.05. The mean and standard deviation are not exactly 50 and 10, respectively, because of the rounding. The complete distribution of T-scores is shown in Figure 3.7.

For the next example, suppose you would like to create a normalized score with a minimum value of 100 and a maximum value of 200. You cannot do this transformation in the *Text Scaling dialog* alone. There is an extra step. You must first create a normalized score in the *Test Scaling dialog* just as we did with normscore (i.e. a normalized score with no linear transformation, truncation, or rounding). Next, start the *Linear Transformation dialog*, and select normscore. Type scalescore as the new variable name, and type 100 in the *Minimum*

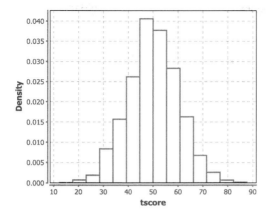

FIGURE 3.7 Histogram of exam2 T-scores

text field and 200 in the *Maximum text field* of the *Constraints panel*. Now click the *Run button*. These steps result in scores that range from 100 to 200 with a mean of 149.99 and a standard deviation of 16.16.

Note

1 Note that the score range in the test scaling descriptive statistics can differ from the score range in the score conversion table. The reason for the difference is that descriptive statistics involve observed values of the scores, whereas the score conversion table involves all possible scores. The score conversion table may include scores not observed in the data.

4

ITEM ANALYSIS

Test development is an extensive and time-consuming process. It includes (a) establishing the purpose of a test, (b) defining the construct of interest, (c) drafting test items, (d) conducting a pilot test, and (e) analyzing item response data. These steps are cyclical in that the analysis of item response data leads to the identification of good items and informs revision of bad ones. Revised items are then subjected to additional rounds of pilot testing and analysis. Several authors provide detailed information about each of these steps (see Crocker & Algina, 1986), but the analysis of item response data is the focus of this and many other chapters in this book. It is an important step in the development of quality measures.

Item analysis is a procedure for quantifying various characteristics of test items. It helps us identify items that are too easy or excessively difficulty for examines, and it aids our understanding of the way an item distinguishes between low- and high-scoring examinees. It is a relatively simple method that has a long tradition in measurement. At its core, item analysis is little more than the computation of means and correlations, but the context of testing leads to specific interpretations of these statistics. *Item difficulty* is the mean item score. For multiple-choice, true/false, and other items that are scored as right (1 point) or wrong (0 points), item difficulty is the proportion of examinees who answered the item correctly. It ranges from 0 to 1, and, despite the name "item difficulty," a large value of this statistic indicates an easy item and a small value indicates a hard item. For example, an item difficulty of 0.8 indicates that 80% of examinees answer the item correctly. On the other hand, an item difficulty of 0.1 shows that only 10% of examinees answer the item correctly. An item with a difficulty of 0.1 is much more difficult than one with a difficulty of 0.8.

Item difficulty for a polytomous item, an item scored in more than two ordinal categories, is simply the item mean or average item score. It ranges between the minimum possible item score and the maximum possible item score. Interpretation of the item difficulty for a polytomous item depends on the minimum and maximum possible item scores. Therefore, a 4-point polytomous item scored as 0, 1, 2, and 3 points has a mean that ranges between 0 and 3 points. The closer the mean is to 0, the more difficult the item (e.g. the harder to achieve the highest category), and the closer the mean is to 3, the easier the item (e.g. the easier it is to attain the highest category).

It is possible to convert the item difficulty for a polytomous item into a proportion correct score by dividing the item mean by the maximum possible item score. For example, suppose an item is scored as 0, 1, 2, and 3 points. An item mean of 2.35 corresponds to a proportion correct score of $2.35/3 = 0.78$. As with binary items, when the polytomous item difficulty is converted to a $0 - 1$ metric, values close to 1 indicate an easy item, and values close to 0 a difficult item. However, it would not be safe to say that 78% of examinees answered this item correctly. This conversion only allows us see that, on average, examinees obtained a large portion of the available points.

The term "item difficulty" makes sense in educational measurement where questions have a correct answer or can be rated on degrees of correctness. In psychological research where the goal is to measure an attitude or personality characteristic, the term is less appropriate. Psychological measures often involve Likert scales that ask people to respond as "Strongly Agree," "Agee," "Disagree," or "Strongly Disagree." There is no correct answer to such a question. Any response is acceptable, and the term "item difficulty" does not apply. For Likert and similar types of items, you can think of the item mean as an index of *item endorsability*— the extent to which the highest response option is endorsed. This term is more consistent with the notion of someone endorsing a particular attitude, where all attitudes are acceptable and none are "correct."

Item discrimination is the extent to which an item differentiates between examinees that obtain different scores on the test. If discrimination is high, the item can easily distinguish between examinees that have similar, but not identical, test scores. On the other hand, if discrimination is low, the item can only distinguish between examinees that have very different test scores. An easy way to quantify discrimination is the D-index. For binary items, it is computed as the difference in item difficulty for the top 27% and bottom 27% of examinees. Large values indicate an item is much easier for top-scoring examinees than it is for low-scoring examinees. The D-index has an intuitive interpretation, and it is easy to compute by hand. Perhaps the main limitation of the D-index is that it does not make use of all available data. The middle 46% of examinees are eliminated from the computation. jMetrik does not use this index. Rather it uses item discrimination statistics that retain all of the available data.

Item discrimination is a correlation between the item score and the total test score. It is often called the item-total correlation for this reason. Pearson's correlation is the most basic type of correlation involved in an item analysis, and it can be applied to binary and polytomous items. It has a different name when it is computed between a binary item and the total test score. In this situation, it is more specifically referred to as a *point-biserial correlation*. There is even a simplified equation for the point-biserial correlation, but it is nothing more than a Pearson correlation. jMetrik item analysis output does not distinguish between a Pearson and point-biserial correlation. It refers to both as a Pearson correlation.

A limitation of the Pearson correlation is its sensitivity to the distribution of examinee ability. If a test involves high ability examinees, it will have a notably different item discrimination value than when the same test is given to a group of low ability examinees. To overcome this limitation, we can assume that a normally distributed latent variable underlies the item score. The correlation between this latent item score and the total test score is referred to as the *biserial correlation* when it is applied to binary items and as the *polyserial correlation* when it is used with polytomous items. Given that the polyserial correlation is the more general form, jMetrik always uses the term polyserial correlation in the item analysis output. The advantage of the polyserial (and biserial) correlation is its stability across different groups of examinees. It will vary less across different groups of examinees (e.g. high-scoring and low-scoring groups) than the Pearson correlation. In addition, the polyserial correlation will always be a little larger than the Pearson correlation.

All item-total correlations have the same interpretation. Positive item-total correlations mean that high-scoring examinees tend to get the item correct, and low-scoring examinees tend to get it wrong. High positive values for the item-total correlation indicate a large amount of discrimination. Values near 0 reflect little to no discrimination. An item-total correlation can take on negative values, but such a result would indicate a problem. It would mean that low-scoring examinees tend to get the item correct. If you ever observe negative item discrimination, check the item itself and the item scoring. You may have provided the wrong answer code, or it could be a reverse-worded item. If the answer key is correct, a negative item discrimination value indicates a serious problem with the item.

Although there are two different types of correlations you can use for an item analysis (i.e. Pearson and polyserial), you should only use one of them. Use either the Pearson or polyserial correlation. Weigh the relative strengths and weaknesses of each type, and choose the one that best suits your needs.

Distractor Analysis

An item analysis takes on a more complete picture when statistics are also computed for the distractors (i.e. the incorrect response options) of a multiple-choice question. The proportion of examinees endorsing a distractor provides information about the plausibility of the distractor. Large values indicate that the distractor attracts many examinees, and small values indicate that few examinees selected the distractor. Proportions close to 0 suggest that the distractor is not functioning, and it is possible to eliminate it as a choice. Distractor proportions close to 1 may indicate an item that is excessively difficult, or it may be a sign of an incorrect answer key.

Distractor-total correlations show the relationship between a distractor and the total test score. They are computed by coding the distractor as 1 point for selected and 0 points for not selected and then correlating this binary distractor score with the total test score. It is either a Pearson or polyserial type correlation, depending on the option you selected for the correlation. We expect to find negative distractor-total correlations because examinees earning higher scores should be less likely to select a distractor. Stated differently, examinees that select a distractor should earn lower overall test scores.

The ideal pattern for a multiple-choice question is to have a positive item discrimination and negative distractor-total correlations. Any deviation from this pattern should be examined closely. Possible explanations for a positive distractor-total correlation include a mistake with the answer key and a distractor that is a legitimate answer. The former can be verified by a review of the answer key and scoring procedures. The latter requires judgment by content area experts. It is possible to have a positive item discrimination and a positive distractor-total correlation. Such an occurrence would indicate that an item does not have a clearly correct answer or that the response options have been stated in an ambiguous manner. The possibility of having a positive distractor-total correlation and a positive item discrimination is the main reason for conducting a distractor analysis. You can only identify this problem through an item analysis that includes all response options.

Item Selection Guidelines

As discussed in chapter 3, in a norm-referenced test, an examinee's score takes on meaning by comparing it to the scores of other examinees. For example, a student that scores in the 90th percentile has a score that is as good as or better than 90% of examinees. This type of test is common in psychology where interest lies in distinguishing between normal and abnormal performance. It is also used in education to identify the best (or worst) students. Norm-referenced tests require individual differences on the measured construct. If everyone were to obtain the same score on the test, this type of interpretation fails. There is no way to rank order examinees when they have the same score. A norm-referenced test should be designed to maximize score variance.

Item difficulty and discrimination are commonly used in conjunction when selecting items for a norm-referenced test. Item discrimination values should be between 0.3 and 0.7, and binary items should have a difficulty value near 0.5. If guessing is a factor, then the ideal difficulty value is slightly more than halfway between chance and 1 (Cronbach & Warrington, 1952; Lord, 1952). For example, a multiple-choice item with four options has an ideal difficulty value that is slightly more than $[0.25 - (1 - 0.25)/2] = 0.625$. These rules of thumb are based on the idea that these values maximize item variance and subsequently increase score reliability. Of course, every item will not likely have an item difficulty that is exactly the ideal value, but items with a difficulty within 0.2 points would be acceptable. For example, for a multiple-choice question in which guessing is not a factor, difficulty values between 0.3 and 0.7 would be acceptably close to the ideal value of 0.5. This range of values will maximize information that the test provides about score differences (Allen & Yen, 1979, p. 121). No comparable rules of thumb exist for polytomous items, but by extension, it is best to select polytomous items that have moderate discrimination values and large item variances.

In a criterion-referenced test, scores are not interpreted relative to the group of examinees. They are interpreted with respect to the content domain and often an absolute standard of performance referred to as a passing score. This type of test is common in education as interest lies in determining which students pass the test and which ones do not. That is, the interest is on mastery of the tested content. For example, a student who earns a score of 85% correct is considered to have mastered about 85% of the content domain. If the passing score was set at 80%, then this student is also considered to have passed the test. It is important to note that every student taking the test can get a score of 85% and pass the test. Since there is no comparison among examinees, it is perfectly acceptable for everyone to achieve the same score. Criterion-referenced tests emphasize the content domain and the passing score; they are not designed to maximize score variability. Consequently, item selection guidelines for a criterion-referenced test differ from a norm-referenced test.

In criterion-referenced testing with a passing score, it is not appropriate to choose items simply for the purpose of maximizing variance (Crocker & Algina, 1986, p. 329). Item selection should account for the passing score and aim to select items that maximize decision consistency (i.e. consistency in the pass/ fail decisions). A variety of alternative item statistics are available for describing the relationship between an item and the passing score, such as the agreement index, B-index, and phi-coefficient. A recent study evaluated the use of these statistics for item selection and compared the results to item selection based on more traditional statistics such as item discrimination. The results showed that the phi-coefficient tended to select easy items and was more dependent on the cut score than item discrimination (Jones, 2011). Moreover, using the phi-coefficient and B-index to select items for a test only improved decision consistency by 1% over item discrimination (Jones, 2009). Taken together, these results suggest that item discrimination is also a useful index for criterion-referenced tests and that choosing items with discrimination values between 0.3 and 0.7 will lead to high levels of decision consistency.

With respect to item difficulty and criterion-referenced tests, an argument can be made for choosing items that span a wide range of difficulties. Examinees of all ability levels will then be able to answer some items, but only accomplished students will be able to answer most of them. As with norm-referenced tests, item difficulty is not the primary consideration when selecting items for a test. Rather, statistics that describe the relationship between the item and total score (or passing score) should have greater weight in the decision to keep or eliminate an item from the test.

After deciding which items to keep and which ones to eliminate from the test, an item analysis should be conducted on the final selection of test items. Eliminating one or more items will change the computation of item discrimination and reliability. It affects item discrimination because the reduced number of items results in different total scores, and it affects reliability by changing the total number of items and observed score variance. If the eliminated items really are bad, reliability could increase even though the final test involves fewer items. The reduction of items could have the opposite effect too. Test length could be shortened to an extent that reduces reliability. You should rerun an item analysis on the final selection of test items to obtain updated estimates of item discrimination and score reliability.

Running the Analysis in jMetrik

Item scoring is a required step before you run an item analysis. It is only after you complete the item scoring that jMetrik will know the difference between a test item and a regular variable. The *Item Analysis dialog* only allows you to select binary and polytomous items. To run the analysis, click **Analyze → Item Analysis** to display the *Item Analysis dialog* (see Figure 4.1).

You can select individual items by clicking an item in the *Unselected list* and then clicking the *Select button*. You could also select multiple items by holding down the CTRL key on a PC (Command + click on a Mac) while clicking items in the *Unselected list*. Pressing the *Select button* will move all of the selected items to the *Selected list*. Alternatively, you can select all of the test items by simply clicking the *Select all button*. Click the *Run button* to execute the analysis. Once the analysis is complete, jMetrik will display a new tab with the results. The item analysis command and any error messages will be recorded in the log. If you would like to save the item statistics to a new table in the database, click the *Save button*, and type a name for the new table in the dialog that appears.

Item Analysis Options

A variety of options listed in the *Item Analysis dialog* give you control over the analysis and resulting output. Three options are selected by default.

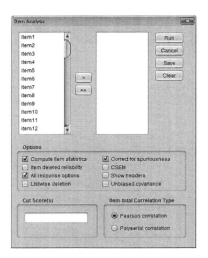

FIGURE 4.1 Item Analysis dialog

- *Compute item statistics*—if selected, jMetrik will compute item statistics such as item difficulty and discrimination. If not selected, jMetrik will only provide reliability estimates and test-level descriptive statistics. This option is selected by default.
- *Item deleted reliability*—if selected, jMetrik will display a table that contains reliability estimates when each item is deleted. The reliability chapter describes the result of this option in more detail.
- *All response options*—if selected, jMetrik will display item statistics for each response option. For the correct answer, these statistics are item difficulty and discrimination. For the distractors, these statistics are the proportion endorsing the distractor and the distractor-total score correlation. If not selected, jMetrik will only display item difficulty and discrimination. This option is selected by default.
- *Listwise deletion*—examinees with missing data are excluded from the analysis when this option is selected. Otherwise, missing data are handled as described in the section on missing data.
- *Correct for spuriousness*—the correlation between an item and the total score is inflated because the item is included in the item score and the total score. jMetrik will adjust for this inflation by removing variance in the total score that is due to the item. This option is selected by default.
- *CSEM*—if selected, jMetrik will provide a table with the conditional standard error of measurement. See the chapter on reliability for more information about this statistic.
- *Show headers*—select this option to have jMetrik display the table header for each item. This option is not selected by default, and the header is only listed once at the beginning of the output.

- Unbiased covariance—item covariances and standard deviations use the total sample size (N) in the denominator resulting in a biased statistic. Select this option to use an unbiased estimator with $N - 1$ in the denominator. For large sample sizes, the effect of this option will be unnoticeable.

In addition to these options, you can provide a list of cut scores in the *Cut score text field* of the *Cut Score(s) panel*. Cut scores must be larger than 0 and less than the maximum possible test score (i.e. total number of points possible for the selected items). Multiple cut scores must be separated by a space. Cut scores are not required, but if you provide them, jMetrik will add a table to the output that contains decision consistency indices (see chapter 5).

Finally, you can choose the type of correlation that is computed between the item (or option) score and the total test score by selecting the desired option in the *Item-total Correlation Type panel*. Choosing *Pearson correlation* will result in a point-biserial correlation for a binary item and a Pearson correlation for a polytomous item. Selecting *Polyserial correlation* will result in a biserial correlation for a binary item and a polyserial correlation for a polytomous item.

A problem with the item-total correlation is that the item is counted in the item score and total test score. Including the item in both the x and y variables of a correlation leads to a spurious value. Although Crocker and Algina (1986) note that including the studied item in the total test score is only a problem for short tests, an adjustment can be applied to the correlation to correct it for spuriousness. The adjustment is given by

$$\rho'_{Xi} = \frac{\rho_{Xi}\sigma_X - \sigma_i}{\sqrt{\sigma_i^2 + \sigma_X^2 - 2\rho_{Xi}\sigma_X\sigma_i}},$$

where ρ_{Xi} is the original correlation between the item and total test score, σ_i is the item standard deviation, σ_X is the total test score standard deviation, and $\rho_{Xi}\sigma_X\sigma_i$ is the covariance between the item and total test score.

Missing Data

jMetrik scores missing, omitted, and not reached item responses as 0 points by default in an item analysis. There is an option for excluding examinees with any missing data by selecting the listwise deletion option. However, listwise deletion is not recommended because it could result in the exclusion of large amounts of data. Item response theory provides a better way of handling missing data whether the excluded responses are coded as missing, omitted, or not reached.

Example 1: Multiple-Choice Items

Example 1 is an analysis of the exam1 data using the default options. A portion of the results are shown in Figure 4.2.

The first column lists the item name, and the second column lists the response options. The option listed as "Overall" contains statistics for the correct answer for a binary item and the overall item mean and item-total correlation for a polytomous item. Other values listed in this column depend on the item scoring. In this example, all items use the options A, B, C, and D. Next to each option is the corresponding point value or score assigned to each option. You can see that option A for item1 is scored as 1 point, and the remaining options are scored as 0 points.

The third column lists item difficulty for the correct answer and the proportion endorsing an option for each distractor. You can see that item1 has a difficulty value of 0.7093 indicating that 71% of examinees selected the correct answer. The least selected distractors were options B and C. Only about 8% of examinees selected each of these distractors.

This fourth column lists the standard deviation. In the row labeled "Overall," this statistic is the item standard deviation. The square of this value is the item variance, and it is useful when selecting items with the largest amount of variance. Rows corresponding to each option display the standard deviation for selecting an option. These rows are not the overall item standard deviation.

Finally, the fifth column of the output contains the item-total and distractor-total correlations. For the "Overall" row, this correlation is the item discrimination statistic. For the other rows, it is simply the correlation between the option score (selected or not) and the total test score. You can see in Figure 4.2 that item1 has an item discrimination of 0.3117 and all distractor-total correlations are negative. Considering these results and the item difficulty statistics, item1 meets the criteria for a good item.

In contrast to item1, item39 fails to meet the criteria (see Figure 4.2). Item difficulty (0.3345) and discrimination (0.2512) are lower than the values we

Item	Option (Score)	Difficulty	Std. Dev.	Discrimin.
item1	Overall	0.7093	0.4541	0.3117
	A(1.0)	0.7093	0.4541	0.3117
	B(0.0)	0.0767	0.2661	-0.2205
	C(0.0)	0.0823	0.2749	-0.2785
	D(0.0)	0.1255	0.3313	-0.1155
item2	Overall	0.5298	0.4992	0.2619
	A(0.0)	0.1430	0.3501	-0.0550
	B(0.0)	0.1485	0.3556	-0.1707
	C(0.0)	0.1710	0.3765	-0.2614
	D(1.0)	0.5298	0.4992	0.2619
...	...	...	...	...
item39	Overall	0.3345	0.4719	0.2512
	A(0.0)	0.1813	0.3853	-0.1187
	B(0.0)	0.2627	0.4401	0.0219
	C(0.0)	0.1858	0.3890	-0.2552
	D(1.0)	0.3345	0.4719	0.2512

FIGURE 4.2 Item analysis output for exam1

would like to have, but the real problem lies in the distractor statistics. Notice that option B has a positive distractor-total correlation (0.0219). This result suggests that high-scoring examinees tend to select this distractor, whereas low-scoring examinees do not. Given that item discrimination is also positive, this item could be ambiguous or have multiple correct answers. It deserves close examination by experts familiar with the item content. Three additional items show this same pattern: `item27`, `item32`, and `item42`. Results for these items highlight the importance of conducting a distractor analysis and not limiting the item analysis to only the correct option. This problem would not have been detected if the analysis focused only on the correct answer.

There are three items that have item-total correlations outside the desired range, but the distractor-total correlations are all negative (see `item28`, `item31`, and `item54`). Although these items are outside the desired range, they are just barely so. Considering the other item statistics, these items are not that bad. We do not want to be too strict in interpreting our rules of thumb, and we do not want to create problems with content validity by eliminating too many items. Moreover, we have already identified four items that exhibit more severe problems, and they should have priority in the decision to remove items from the analysis.

Two of the items that had a distractor with a positive distractor-total correlation also had item-total correlations outside the desired range. We can eliminate `item27` and `item32` from the analysis and evaluate the effect on the remaining items. Figure 4.3 shows the *Item Analysis dialog* with these two items not selected for the analysis. Clicking the *Run button* will execute the analysis without these two items.

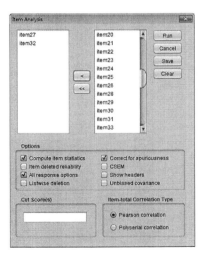

FIGURE 4.3 Item Analysis dialog with two items removed from the analysis

It is important to check the item-total and distractor-total correlations after omitting items from an analysis. In the process of conducting the item analysis, jMetrik computes a total score based on the selected items. It is this total score that is correlated with an item to produce item-total and distractor-total correlations. If you decide to exclude an item from the analysis, the total score will be different than it would have been with the item included. Consequently, all of the item-total and distractor-total correlations will change when you exclude an item from the analysis. Check the correlations again to make sure they continue to meet the criteria for a good item.

You can save the item analysis statistics to a new database table by clicking the *Save button* to display the *New Table Name dialog.* As shown in Figure 4.4, type a name in the text field and click the *OK button* to accept the new table name. After you execute the analysis, a new table will be added to the database, and the name will appear in the list of table names.

Click the new table name in the list to display the results (Figure 4.5). With this table selected, you can produce descriptive statistics for your item analysis. For example, you can compute the range and mean for item difficulty and discrimination. Using all of the items for the exam1 analysis, we see that item difficulty ranges from 0.1630 to 0.8555 with an average value of 0.5420. This range is a little larger than we would like, but the average is close to the ideal value for a norm-referenced test. Item discrimination values range from 0.1765 to 0.5832 with an average value of 0.3759. This range and average value is on the low side, perhaps because these results include `item27` and `item32`.

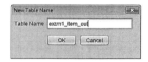

FIGURE 4.4 New Table Name dialog

name	difficulty	stdev	discrimination
item1	0.7093	0.4541	0.3117
item2	0.5298	0.4992	0.2619
item3	0.8118	0.3909	0.4112
item4	0.5735	0.4946	0.2387
item5	0.6528	0.4761	0.2948
item6	0.7328	0.4425	0.3493
item7	0.4597	0.4984	0.3207

FIGURE 4.5 Example output table from an item analysis

Example 2: Likert Scale Items

Example 2 is an analysis of the exam2 data. These data are from a test composed of all Likert scale items that are scored from 0 to 3 points. The item selection rules for polytomous items apply for these data, but the steps for running the analysis are a little different. The main difference concerns the distractors. Likert items do not have distractors in the sense that there are wrong answers. All values are acceptable. As such, it is difficult to prescribe the desired direction of the option-total correlation for all of the response options. For this reason, the analysis will only focus on the overall item rather than the distractors. Run the analysis in the same way as example 1, but unselect the checkbox for *All response options*. The output will then only display statistics for the whole item.

Results for the exam2 item analysis are displayed in Figure 4.6. Notice that item difficulty is no longer restricted to the range from 0 to 1. The items are scored from 0 to 3. Therefore, the closer the item difficulty is to 3, the easier the item. You can see in the figure that `item18` is the easiest item (2.5940) and `item10` is the most difficult (1.1120). Dividing each of these values by the maximum possible item score puts item difficulty back onto a 0 to 1 scale, but the interpretation is different than it was for binary items. Item difficulty values for `item18` and `item10` become 0.8647 and 0.3707, respectively, when divided by the maximum possible item score. With this transformation it is easy to see that `item18` is easier than `item10`.

With respect to item discrimination, the estimates range from 0.4971 to 0.6548 and are clearly in the desired range. There is no indication of a problem with any of these items.

All of the items in the first example were binary, and all of the items in the second example were polytomous. Do not take these examples to mean that your test can contain only one item type. jMetrik can also analyze data from a mixed

Item	Option (Score)	Difficulty	Std. Dev.	Discrimin.
item1	Overall	2.1540	1.0219	0.5342
item2	Overall	1.4280	1.1780	0.6168
item3	Overall	1.2880	0.8687	0.5173
item4	Overall	1.2260	1.0398	0.5819
item5	Overall	2.2020	1.0331	0.5814
item6	Overall	1.1320	1.0318	0.5447
item7	Overall	1.5720	1.1346	0.6241
item8	Overall	2.1820	0.8380	0.5251
item9	Overall	1.2900	1.1386	0.6065
item10	Overall	1.1120	1.0797	0.5941
item11	Overall	1.2340	1.0457	0.5981
item12	Overall	1.3860	1.0154	0.5513
item13	Overall	1.2360	1.1255	0.6265
item14	Overall	1.1560	1.0891	0.5719
item15	Overall	1.1940	0.9392	0.5401
item16	Overall	1.3400	0.9891	0.5969
item17	Overall	1.8420	1.0350	0.5533
item18	Overall	2.5940	0.6856	0.4971
item19	Overall	1.4000	1.0149	0.5756
item20	Overall	1.4400	1.1085	0.6548

FIGURE 4.6 Exam2 item analysis results

format test, which is a test that contains binary and polytomous items. If you are analyzing data from a mixed format test, be sure to select *All response options* in the item analysis dialog so that you can see the distractor statistics for the binary items. Choosing that option will also display distractor statistics for the polytomous items, but you can ignore that information and focus on the results for the overall item.

5

RELIABILITY

In a basic sense, reliability refers to the reproducibility of test scores. Imagine repeating a test over and over again and the only thing that changes with each administration is the selection of items on the test. Each set of items (i.e. each test form) represents a different way of measuring the same construct. They all conform to the same test specifications and measure the same content, but the specific items are different. We expect scores to change a little with each test form because of the different items on each one. However, we hope they do not change very much because that would adversely affect measurement of the construct and greatly increase the chance of making incorrect decisions about examinee performance. The extent to which scores from each form are similar is reflected in the reliability coefficient. If reliability is high, we can be assured that test scores from one test form will be similar to score from another. Reliable test scores are reproducible test scores.

Classical Test Theory

Classical test theory is an approach to measurement that provides a definition of reliability and methods for estimating reliability. It primarily concerns norm-referenced tests, where the goal of test design is to capitalize on individual differences and create a test that taps into this heterogeneity. As implied by the name, it is one of the oldest theories of test scores. Classical test theory originated with Charles Spearman's work on measurement error in the early 1900s (Spearman, 1904, 1910), and more formal developments arose over the years with notable contributions described in classic texts by Gulliksen (1950) and Lord and Novick (1968).

To conceptualize classical test theory, imagine a universe or collection of all possible test items that measure the construct of interest. This universe is typically defined by a theoretical framework or table of specifications that defines the construct, test content, and other aspects of the measurement procedure such as the administration procedures and supplemental materials needed for testing (e.g. calculators). All of the possible test items need not actually exist, but through a clear definition of the universe, we would know which items belong to it and which ones do not.

The test form we actually create is considered to be just one possible test form we could have created from the universe. That is, it represents one realization of a random process. There are many other tests that could be created by randomly sampling other items that tap into our construct, but the test we actually give to examinees is just one of these possibilities. The score an examinee earns on a particular test is an observed score. It is a value we observe by adding up the number of points awarded for each item.

If we were to create another test form by sampling a new set of items from the universe, an examinee would not likely get the exact same observed score as the previous test. It would be different because the new test form might be easier or more difficult than the old test form. Now, imagine repeating this process a large number of times—sampling items from the universe, administering the test to an examinee, and computing an observed score. An examinee would then have a distribution of observed scores that characterize the variability associated with sampling items from the universe. The average value of this distribution is an examinee's true score, and the difference between an observed score and the true score is an error score. More specifically, the classical test theory model is $X = T + E$, where X is the observed score, T is the true score, and E is the error score. Because each examinee has a (theoretical) distribution of observed scores, each examinee also has a (theoretical) distribution of error scores. The mean of the examinee-specific error score distribution is 0, and its variance is the same as the examinee-specific observed score distribution. Classical test theory is fully defined with some additional assumptions: (a) the test measures a single construct (i.e. it is unidimensional), (b) errors scores from one test are unrelated to error scores from another test, and (c) true scores are unrelated to error scores.

It is rarely the case that we actually repeat the measurement procedure multiple times. A test is almost always given once. As such, we never actually obtain person-specific observed score distributions, but we do obtain a distribution of observed scores for the group of examinees taking the test. We can compute the observed score variance for the group of examinees and denote it as $\sigma^2(X)$. When the assumptions of classical test theory hold true, this variance can be decomposed into true score variance and error variance, $\sigma^2(X) = \sigma^2(T) + \sigma^2(E)$. This decomposition leads to a definition of the reliability coefficient,

$$\rho_{XT}^2 = \frac{\sigma^2(T)}{\sigma^2(T) + \sigma^2(E)}.$$

The notation for the reliability coefficient indicates that it represents the squared correlation between observed and true scores. It represents the amount of observed score variance that is explained by true scores. Values for the reliability coefficient range from 0 to 1. Values close to 1 are better and indicate that a large portion of observed score variance is due to true scores. Stated differently, a high reliability coefficient means that observed scores are very reproducible because they are mainly due to the true score. Conversely, values near 0 indicate that most of the observed score variance is due to measurement error; we cannot easily reproduce observed scores because they are mainly due to random error.

In a practical testing situation, we only obtain the observed scores, but we would like to make decisions based on the true scores. The value of the reliability coefficient is that it reflects the extent to which variance among observed scores is similar to the variance among true scores. When reliability is 1, there is no error variance, and we will obtain the same rank ordering with observed scores as we would with true scores. For a given level of true score variance, the reliability coefficient will tend toward 0 as error variance increases. With an extremely large amount of error variance, reliability will be close to 0, and we would be unlikely to obtain the same rank ordering with observed scores as we would with true scores. Thus, the reliability coefficient tells us how much confidence we can have in decisions based on observed scores.

Sources of Measurement Error

The discussion of reliability thus far has focused on only one source of measurement error—the selection of test items. However, there are many sources of error that affect test scores. Examples include the occasion of testing and internal examinee characteristics such as fatigue, motivation, and effort. Other factors such as raters for subjectively scored tests (e.g. performance assessments) and mode of test administration can also be important sources of measurement error.

Estimation of Reliability

A limitation of classical test theory is that it only describes one source of measurement error. There is only one E in the classical model. It is not possible to use a single model to describe multiple sources of measurement error in classical test theory. Therefore, we must use a variety of reliability estimates to describe the influence of different sources of measurement error. Each type of estimate uses a different data collection design to isolate the influence of a different source of measurement error.

An alternate forms reliability estimate is obtained by creating two tests that are similar in all aspects (e.g. content, difficulty, reliability, and standard deviation) except for the actual test items that comprise each form. Examinees complete both forms in a counterbalanced fashion. During the first administration, half of the examinees complete Form A, and the other examinees complete Form B. Within a very short period of time, perhaps the same or the following day, examinees sit for a second exam. Examinees who originally completed Form A now take Form B, and those who originally completed Form B now take form A. An estimate of reliability is obtained by correlating the Form A and Form B scores. Given that test items are the only difference between the two forms, the main source of error described by this estimate is the selection of test items. Therefore, an alternate forms reliability estimate is referred to as a coefficient of equivalence. It is consistent with the item sampling process described earlier in the chapter.

To evaluate the temporal stability of scores, we can use a test-retest reliability estimate. Data collection for this estimate involves administering the test to examinees and then administering the same test to the same examinees three weeks later. An estimate of reliability is obtained by correlating the scores from the first administration to the scores from the second. A high correlation indicates that scores are stable over time, whereas a low correlation implies that scores are not stable and subject to random fluctuations over time. The test-retest coefficient is referred to as a coefficient of stability in recognition that it relates to random score changes, or lack thereof, over time.

The main problem with alternate forms and test-retest reliability is that examinees must take two exams. For a large-scale educational exam that costs test developers millions of dollars to create and examinees several hours to complete, giving a test twice simply for the purpose of estimating reliability is unreasonable, if not completely inhumane. Therefore, alternative methods for estimating reliability are necessary.

A split-half reliability estimate requires only a single test administration. After examinees complete the exam, it is divided into two halves, and the half-test scores are correlated. Given that correlation coefficients are affected by a restriction in range, it is necessary to adjust the half-test correlation to account for the full length of the test. This adjustment is achieved with the Spearman-Brown formula (Brown, 1910; Spearman, 1910), which is given by $SB = 2r/(1+r)$, where r is the half-test correlation. For a half-test correlation of 0.6, the Spearman-Brown estimate is 0.75.

Internal consistency estimates of reliability are an alternative to split-half methods. They use inter-item covariances to produce an estimate of reliability. They are referred to as internal consistency estimates because they reflect how well items hang together. A common misconception about internal consistency is that these estimates reflect the extent to which a measure is unidimensional. That is, people often confuse a high internal consistency estimate as an indication that the test measures only one thing. Tests that measure multiple dimensions can also produce high internal consistency estimates. Therefore, the proper interpretation is to consider them a measure of the similarity among items. If there is a high degree of similarity, then items will produce consistent scores.

The earliest internal consistency methods date back to work by Kuder and Richardson (1937) who developed a number of methods including the KR20 and KR21. These two methods are limited to binary items, but the KR21 makes the additional assumption that items are equally difficult. Guttman (1945) expanded on their work and developed six lower bounds to reliability. His third lower bound (L3) is better known as coefficient alpha, and it generalizes the KR20 to binary and polytomous items. Stated differently, coefficient alpha and the KR20 produce the same result when items are binary. Coefficient alpha is given by

$$\text{Coefficient } \alpha = \left(\frac{k}{k-1} \right) \left(\frac{\sigma_X^2 - \sum_{j=1}^{k} \sigma_{X_j}^2}{\sigma_X^2} \right).$$

Guttman's third lower bound is a simplification of his second lower bound (L2). However, his second lower bound is actually a better lower bound to reliability. L2 will always be equal to or greater than coefficient alpha (L3). Guttman's second lower bound is given by the following equation:

$$\text{L2} = \left(\frac{\sqrt{\frac{k}{k-1} \left[\sigma_X^4 - \sum_{j=1}^{k} \sigma_{X_j}^4 \right]}}{\sigma_X^2} \right) + \left(\frac{\sigma_X^2 - \sum_{j=1}^{k} \sigma_{X_j}^2}{\sigma_X^2} \right).$$

It is interesting to note that some authors refer to coefficient alpha as "Cronbach's alpha" and cite his 1951 article in *Psychometrika*. Although Cronbach's 1951 article made several unique contributions to psychometrics, coefficient alpha was not one of them. He even acknowledged coefficient alpha had a different origin and should not be called "Cronbach's alpha" (Cronbach & Shavelson, 2004). Two of the other contributions from Cronbach's 1951 paper are noteworthy here. First, Cronbach showed that coefficient alpha was the average of all possible split-halves. Consequently, there is no longer reason to choose a way to split a test into halves. Coefficient alpha will be the average of all possible ways. Second,

Cronbach demonstrated that coefficient alpha can be high even when a test measures multiple dimensions. Thus, he warned that it should never be interpreted as an indication that a test measures only one thing. Although Cronbach did not invent coefficient alpha, he furthered our understanding of the method. Recognizing the contribution of both authors to our understanding of coefficient alpha, McDonald refers to it as "Guttman-Cronbach alpha" (McDonald, 1999, p. 92).

Methods for estimating reliability make different assumptions about the relationships among scores, and these affect the interpretation of an estimate. Many estimates are based on the assumption that scores are parallel. Lord and Novick described this assumption as having scores that "measure exactly the same thing in the same scale and, in a sense, measure it equally well for all persons" (1968, p. 48). Alternate forms and the Spearman-Brown formula are two methods based on this assumption. However, it is a very strict assumption that is unlikely to be met in practice. Tau-equivalence relaxes the assumption of parallel measures by allowing scores to have different error variances. Essential tau-equivalence further relaxes the assumption by allowing for unequal error variances and different mean scores. The least strict assumption is that scores are congeneric. Congeneric measures (Jöreskog, 1971) allow for different score means, error variances, and relationships with the latent trait. It is arguably the most tenable assumption in practice. Coefficient alpha estimates reliability when scores are at least essentially tau-equivalent, but when scores are congeneric, coefficient alpha is only a lower bound to reliability. Guttman's coefficients were all developed under a relaxed set of assumptions and should always be considered to be lower bounds.

There are other measures of internal consistency that were developed under the assumption of congeneric or classically congeneric measures. Two of these methods are provided in jMetrik. Feldt and Gilmer (Feldt, 1975; Gilmer & Feldt, 1983) developed a measure of internal consistency using an assumption of classically congeneric measures. It is an assumption like congeneric measures but with the added restriction that error variances be proportional to effective test length. The Feldt-Gilmer coefficient is difficult to compute and can only be computed when tests have more than two parts (e.g. more than two items). An easier method of computing a reliability estimate for classically congeneric measures is the Feldt-Brennan (Feldt & Brennan, 1989) coefficient.

Standard Error of Measurement

The standard error of measurement (SEM) is the square root of the expected value of the person-specific error variances. We estimate the SEM by $SEM = \sigma(X)\sqrt{1 - \rho_{XT}^2}$, where $\sigma(X)$ is the standard deviation of observed scores for a group of examinees. Any acceptable estimate of reliability may be substituted for the reliability coefficient, ρ^2_{XT}, to compute the SEM. A benefit of the SEM is that it quantifies error variability in the scale of the measure itself. It tells us how far off we expect scores to be using the scale of our measure. Coupled with an assumption of normally distributed scores, a 95% confidence interval for the true score is obtained by $X \pm 1.96(\text{SEM})$. Thus, we can obtain a range of values within which we expect to find an examinee's true score.

The downside of the SEM is that it depends on the scale of measurement. We cannot use it to compare the quality of measures that use different scales. We cannot even use it to compare a measure to a shortened version of the same measure because shortening a test changes the observed score scale [i.e. $\sigma(X)$]. We must use a reliability estimate to compare measures that are on different scale because the reliability coefficient is scale free. The *Standards for Educational and Psychological Testing* (American Educational Research Association, American Psychological Association, & National Council on Measurement in Education, 1999) recommends reporting the SEM and one or more estimates of reliability. This practice capitalizes on the benefits associated with the SEM and the reliability coefficient.

Factors That Affect Reliability

The reliability coefficient is affected by several factors. As evident in the equation for the reliability coefficient, reliability will be larger for heterogeneous populations [i.e. large values of $\sigma^2(T)$], and it will be smaller for homogenous populations [i.e. small values of $\sigma^2(T)$]. This factor is a reason for reporting a reliability estimate for different subgroups of examinees (American Educational Research Association et al., 1999). For example, males may be more heterogeneous than female examinees. As a result, reliability will be higher for males than it will be for females. Reporting an estimate for each group is necessary to ensure that reliability is at an acceptable level for all examinees.

As second factor that affects reliability is test length. All other things being equal, longer tests are more reliable than shorter tests. This relationship is evident in the Spearman-Brown formula, which shows the increase in reliability that arises from doubling test length. An important caveat to note is that reliability will not increase by adding any arbitrary item to the test. The new items must be like the ones already on the test.

Two other factors that affect reliability are related to the underlying assumptions of classical test theory: dimensionality and uncorrelated errors. Unidimensionality requires that a test measures one and only one construct. If a test measures multiple constructs (whether intentionally or not), reliability will be underestimated. That is, reliability will be a lower bound when multiple dimensions affect test scores. The assumption of unrelated error scores means that our test items are independent. An examinee's response to one question does not affect her response to another one. This assumption tends to be violated in practical testing situations. It may be violated under conditions of test speededness, which occurs when a test's time limit is too strict and examinees change their response behavior near the end of a test. It may also be violated when a test contains groups of related items such as a group of items that ask questions about a common reading passage or a group of math items that pertain to a shared graph or figure. These groups of related items are called testlets (see Wainer, Bradlow, & Wang, 2007), and they are like a test within a test. The effect of correlated errors on reliability estimation is less predictable than the effect of multidimensionality. In some cases, correlated errors will overestimate reliability (Zimmerman, Zumbo, & LaLonde, 1993), and in other cases, they will under estimate it (Green & Hershberger, 2000).

Binomial Error Models and the Conditional SEM

A limitation of classical test theory is that true scores are required to be unrelated to error scores, and we only obtain a single, overall SEM. Given that the SEM is based on an average of person-specific error variance, it is a value that represents some people well but others less accurately. Strong true score theory provides an alternative framework that results in a conditional SEM (CSEM). That is, it allows us to compute the SEM at different true scores. This development is important in the context of criterion-referenced testing. It allows you to evaluate the SEM at specific cut scores, rather than some overall value.

Strong true score theory is one way of obtaining standard errors at specific score levels. Early developments employ binomial error models, whereas more recent treatments use item response theory. Binomial error models assume that an examinee with a domain score (i.e. true score) of π_i has an observed score distribution for an N item test that is binomial with parameters N and π_i. The domain score can be estimated from the data as the proportion of items answered correctly by an examinee (Subkoviak, 1976), or domain scores can be assumed to follow a beta distribution or some other distribution of scores. When domain scores follow a beta distribution and the conditional distribution of observed scores is binomial, the marginal distribution of observed scores is beta-binomial (Keats & Lord, 1962) with parameters that take into account test length and score reliability (see Meyer, 2010). Using a binomial error model, Keats developed a CSEM given by

$$CSEM(\pi) = \sqrt{\frac{1 - \rho_{XT}^2}{1 - r_{21}} \left[\frac{\pi(N - \pi)}{N - 1} \right]},$$

where ρ_{XT}^2 is the reliability coefficient and r_{21} is the KR21 (Kuder & Richardson, 1937). An estimate of reliability such as coefficient alpha may be substituted for the reliability coefficient. jMetrik uses this method of computing the CSEM. It is suitable for tests composed of binary items. jMetrik also provides this computation for tests composed of polytomous or mixed item formats by letting N represent the total number of points instead of the total number of items. The reasoning behind this extension to nonbinary items is that polytomous items may be viewed as multiple binary items (Huynh, 1996; Wilson, 1988). However, other methods specifically designed for computing the CSEM for polytomous and mixed format tests (Lee, 2007) are more appropriate but not currently available in jMetrik.

Decision Consistency Indices

In a criterion-referenced framework, the focus of reliability concerns whether or not we would make the same pass/fail decision if the test were replicated. Returning to the concept of repeating the measurement procedure over and over again, a consistent decision is made whenever an examinee fails every time the test is repeated. A consistent decision is also made whenever an examinee passes every repetition of the test. Errors are made when an examinee fails some repetitions of the test but passes others. These errors represent inconsistent decisions.

As described earlier, repeating the test many times does not actually occur, but to estimate decision consistency, we need at least two replications of the measurement procedure. As done when computing alternate forms reliability, two very similar tests can be constructed and given to examinees. A raw agreement index can be computed by summing the number of examinees who pass both tests or fail both tests and dividing this number by the total number of examinees. This statistic would be 0 when everyone fails one test but passes the other (or vice versa). It would be one when all of the examinees pass both tests or fail both tests.

A limitation of the raw agreement index is that it does not account for chance levels of agreement. That is, we expect to have a certain amount of agreement that is due to chance and not the quality of a test. Cohen (1960) developed an alternative statistic that adjusts for chance levels of agreement. His kappa statistic is typically smaller than the raw agreement index, but it has a different interpretation. For example, a kappa statistic of 0.3 is interpreted as a 30% improvement beyond chance. Compared to the raw agreement index, 0.3 seems small, but a 30% improvement beyond chance is a substantial gain.

Raw agreement and kappa statistics are rarely used in practical testing situations because they require examinees to take two tests. Thankfully, researchers have created methods for estimating these statistics from a single test administration. In particular, Huynh (1976a, 1976b) developed methods based on the assumption that scores from one test follow a beta-binomial distribution and that scores from a second, hypothetical test follow the same beta-binomial distribution. Consequently, scores from both tests follow a bivariate beta-binomial distribution. Estimates of raw agreement and kappa may then be obtained from the bivariate beta-binomial distribution. Interpretation of Huynh's raw agreement and kappa statistics are the same as described earlier. The only difference is that his methods involve a hypothetical replication of the test. Huynh's raw agreement and kappa statistics use the beta-binomial and bivariate beta-binomial distributions. The former is given by

$$h(x) = \binom{N}{x} \frac{B(x+\alpha, n-x+\beta)}{B(\alpha,\beta)},$$

where $\alpha = (-1+1/r_{21})\hat{\mu}_x$ and $\beta = -\alpha + Nr_{21} - N$. The bivariate beta-binomial is

$$f(x,y) = \frac{\binom{N}{x}\binom{N}{y}}{B(\alpha,\beta)} B(\alpha + x + y, 2N + \beta - x - y).$$

Notice that the parameters for the beta-binomial and bivariate beta-binomial are the same. Thus, α and β can be computed from a single test administration. Huynh's raw agreement index for the $l = 1, \ldots, L$ cut scores, C_l, is given by

$$P_{Huynh} = \sum_{l=1}^{L} \sum_{x,y=C_{l-1}}^{C_l-1} f(x,y).$$

Chance agreement can be computed from the beta-binomial distribution using

$$P_{Huynh-chance} = \sum_{l=1}^{L} \left[\sum_{x=c_{l-1}}^{C_l-1} h(x) \right]^2.$$

Huynh's kappa is then

$$\kappa_{Huynh} = \frac{P_{Huynh} - P_{Huynh-chance}}{1 - P_{Huynh-chance}}.$$

jMetrik computes Huynh's raw agreement and kappa statistics when you provide cut scores in the *Cut Score(s) panel* of the *Item Analysis dialog*. They are listed in a table that is labeled "Decision Consistency." Other methods for estimating decision consistency from a single test administration exist but are not currently implemented in jMetrik. These alternatives include an extension of Huynh's work to the compound beta-binomial distribution (Hanson &

Brennan, 1990), an agreement statistic that assumes two independent binomial distributions (Subkoviak, 1976), and nonparametric methods that make no distributional assumptions at all (Brennan & Wan, 2004). All of these methods, including Hyunh's, are designed for binary items only. As noted for the CSEM, there is a basis for using these method with polytomous items or a combination of binary and polytomous items, but methods developed specifically for polytomous items or mixed format tests are preferable. Lee, Brennan, and Wan (2009) recently developed a decision consistency method for tests involving polytomous items, but it is not currently available in jMetrik.

Running the Analysis in jMetrik

Reliability analysis is integrated into the item analysis procedure in jMetrik. Every time you run an item analysis, jMetrik will provide reliability estimates for the selected items. As described in chapter 4, click **Analyze → Item Analysis** to display the *Item Analysis dialog*. Select the items you would like to include in the analysis, and click the *OK button*. A table listed at the end of the item analysis output contains the reliability estimates for five different measures of internal consistency: (a) Guttman's L2, (b) coefficient alpha, (c) Feldt-Gilmer, (d) Feldt-Brennan, and (e) Raju's beta. Along with each estimate is a 95% confidence interval and SEM value. Confidence intervals are based on the F-distribution, and they are only accurate for coefficient alpha (Feldt, Woodruff, & Salih, 1987). Confidence intervals for the other methods are only approximations at best because their sampling distribution is unknown.

Reliability Analysis Options

Three options in the item analysis dialog affect the reliability analysis and subsequent output. You can tell jMetrik to only display results for the reliability analysis by unselecting the option for *Compute item statistics*. Only the Reliability Analysis table (see Figure 5.1) will be displayed when this option is unselected.

The second option that affects the reliability analysis is the option for *Item deleted reliability*. If you select this option, an additional table is added to the output. The first column of this table lists the item names and the remaining columns list reliability estimates for the different reliability methods. The reliability methods are Guttman's L2, coefficient alpha (Alpha), Feldt-Gilmer (F-G), Feldt-Brennan (F-B), and Raju's beta (Raju), respectively. Values listed in the table are reliability estimates that exclude the item listed at the beginning of the row in which the estimate is listed. To interpret the values in the Reliability if Item Deleted table, choose a measure of internal consistency, and compare each estimate to the estimate listed for the same internal consistency measure listed in the Reliability Analysis table. If the item deleted reliability estimate is larger than the overall estimate, consider removing the item from the test because doing so will increase reliability. Keep in mind that the Reliability if Item Deleted table is only good for selecting one item to remove from the test. You cannot use it to select multiple items for removal. You must repeat this analysis after removing an item from the test in order to identify the next item to remove.

The third option is *CSEM*. Selecting this option tells jMetrik to compute the CSEM. It will be computed at all true score values between 0 and the maximum possible test score. A table with the true score and CSEM values will be added to the item analysis output when this option is selected.

Finally, a user can provide one or more cut scores in the *Cut Score(s) panel* of the *Item Analysis dialog*. Cut scores must be within the range of 0 to the maximum possible test score. Values outside this range will generate an error. Multiple cut scores must be separated by a space. If you supply one or more cut scores, jMetrik will add a table to the output with Huynh's raw agreement and kappa statistics for decision consistency. The table will also contain standard errors and confidence intervals for the decision consistency indices.

Missing Data

Missing data in a reliability analysis are handled in the same manner as an item analysis. See chapter 4 for details.

Example 1: Multiple-Choice Items

The initial reliability analysis includes all of the exam1 items and the option to compute *Item deleted reliability* estimates. As shown in Figure 5.1, coefficient alpha is 0.9106, and the SEM is 3.2915. With 95% confidence, the reliability coefficient lies between 0.9074 and 0.9138. These results indicate that true scores account for about 91% of the variability in observed scores.

Notice that the estimate for Guttman's L2 is larger than the estimate for coefficient alpha. It is a better lower bound to reliability, and it will always be larger than coefficient alpha. For this reason, Guttman's L2 is a better measure of internal consistency than coefficient alpha. Unfortunately, it is less well-known, and few people actually use it. In this example, both estimates are the same when rounded

```
                       RELIABILIY ANALYSIS
==================================================================
Method              Estimate      95% Conf. Int.            SEM
------------------------------------------------------------------
Guttman's L2         0.9119       (0.9087, 0.9151)         3.2670
Coefficient Alpha    0.9106       (0.9074, 0.9138)         3.2915
Feldt-Gilmer         0.9117       (0.9085, 0.9149)         3.2711
Feldt-Brennan        0.9115       (0.9083, 0.9147)         3.2753
Raju's Beta          0.9106       (0.9074, 0.9138)         3.2915
```

FIGURE 5.1 Reliability estimates, confidence intervals, and SEMs for exam1

to the nearest hundredth. Therefore, we use the more familiar coefficient alpha. Also notice that for these data, the Feldt-Gilmer and Feldt-Brennan methods are larger than coefficient alpha. These two estimators will not always be larger than coefficient alpha, but in this case, they are.

In chapter 5, we identified exam1 items that appeared problematic, and we decided to eliminate `item27` and `item32` from the analysis. To determine the effect of removing these items on score reliability, we will run the analysis without them. As shown in Figure 5.2, eliminating these items increased coefficient alpha from 0.9106 to 0.9110. It is a small change, but reliability did not decrease when we shortened the test by two items. This result provides additional support for removing these two items.

Of the other items that we flagged as problematic, only one item results in an increase in reliability when removed from the test (item deleted reliability output not shown). Coefficient alpha increases ever so slightly from 0.9110 to 0.9111 when `item31` is removed. This improvement is negligible and not worth risking problems with content validity. Therefore, we will retain `item31`.

Before we make the final decision to remove any item from the test, we must evaluate the impact of this decision on content validity. Does removing items have a negative effect on test content? Does the distribution of items in the shortened test substantially differ from the distribution of items listed in the table of specifications? If test content is adversely affected, then the small gains in reliability seen here do not justify removal of `item27` and `item32`. In an ideal scenario, you would have a pool of good items that measure the same content as these two items, and you could select items from this pool as replacements.

For the sake of example, suppose that a cut score of 42 points is set for the final selection of 54 items on an exam (all items except `item27` and `item32`). Examinees earning fewer than 42 points do not pass the test, but those earning 42 or more points do. To evaluate reliability for this criterion-referenced interpretation, we will type 42 in the *Cut Score(s) panel* of the *Item Analysis dialog* so that jMetrik will produce estimates of decision consistency. As shown in Figure 5.3, Huynh's raw agreement index and kappa statistics are 0.91 and 0.67, respectively. This result indicates that 91% of examinees are correctly classified when using a cut score of 42. This level of agreement is a 67% improvement over chance levels of agreement.

```
                          RELIABILITY ANALYSIS
================================================================
Method              Estimate      95% Conf. Int.        SEM
----------------------------------------------------------------
Guttman's L2        0.9121       (0.9089, 0.9153)      3.2140
Coefficient Alpha   0.9110       (0.9077, 0.9142)      3.2351
Feldt-Gilmer        0.9119       (0.9087, 0.9151)      3.2180
Feldt-Brennan       0.9117       (0.9085, 0.9149)      3.2218
Raju's Beta         0.9110       (0.9077, 0.9142)      3.2351
----------------------------------------------------------------
```

FIGURE 5.2 Reliability results for exam1 without bad items

```
                    DECISION CONSISTENCY
================================================================
Huynh's Raw Agreement Index = 0.91
        Standard Error of Agreement: 0.00
        95% Conf. Int. of Agreement: (0.91, 0.92)
Huynh's Kappa = 0.67
        Standard Error of Kappa: 0.00
        95% Conf. Int. of Kappa: (0.67, 0.68)
KR-21: 0.90
Beta-binomial alpha: 3.20
Beta-binomial beta: 2.59
```

FIGURE 5.3 Decision consistency estimates

```
CONDITIONAL STANDARD ERROR OF MEASUREMENT
================================================================
True Score                CSEM
----------------------------------------------------------------
         0               0.0
         1               0.95
         2               1.33
         3               1.61
         4               1.85
         5               2.04
         6               2.22
         7               2.37
         8               2.51
         9               2.63
        10               2.74
       ...               ...
        42               2.93
        43               2.84
        44               2.74
        45               2.63
        46               2.51
        47               2.37
        48               2.22
        49               2.04
        50               1.85
        51               1.61
        52               1.33
        53               0.95
        54               0.0
----------------------------------------------------------------
```

FIGURE 5.4 CSEM output

Finally, selecting the *CSEM* option produces a table for the CSEM. Using the 54 best items, the CSEM at a cut score of 42 is 2.93, which is slightly smaller than the overall SEM of 3.24. A portion of this table is shown in Figure 5.4. Notice that the CSEM takes on the largest values near the average test score, and that CSEM values decrease toward the extreme scores (i.e. scores of 0 and the maximum possible test score). This pattern reinforces the idea that errors are related to true scores such that errors are larger for central true scores but smaller for more extreme true scores.

Example 2: Likert Scale Items

In chapter 5, our analysis of the exam2 data did not identify any items for removal. All of the items met our criteria for a good test item. Coefficient alpha for the complete test is 0.9185, and the true value of the reliability coefficient is between 0.9077 and 0.9285, with 95% confidence. The SEM is 3.6694. Assuming that scores are normally distributed, we can be 95% confident that an examinee's true score lies within 7.2 points of the observed score (i.e. $X \pm 1.96[3.6694]$) on a scale that ranges from 0 to 60.

To further evaluate whether removing an item would improve reliability, we can run the analysis with the *Item deleted reliability* option selected. Figure 5.5 shows that there is no item that when removed will increase the reliability estimate. For example, removing `item1` will lower coefficient alpha to 0.9154, and removing `item2` will lower it to 0.9136. These results confirm our decision to retain all of the items. They are all good items.

Finally, we will compute a split-half reliability estimate to see how it compares to the internal consistency estimates. This analysis in only done here for demonstration purposes. We will use an odd/even split for the computation. The first step is to use the test scaling procedure to compute the half-test scores. Using this method, we computed a set of scores for the odd items and another set of scores for the even items. Next, we use the correlation analysis in jMetrik to obtain a correlation between the odd/even half-test scores. The result is a correlation of 0.8549. Using the Spearman-Brown formula, the estimated split-half reliability is 0.9218, which is larger than the original coefficient alpha of 0.9198. Recall that coefficient alpha is the average of all possible split-halves. Therefore, some split-half values will be larger than it, and others will be smaller. Indeed, repeating the analysis with a first-half/second-half split results in a split-half estimate of 0.9192, a value slightly smaller than the original coefficient alpha.

Another way to compute part-test reliability coefficients is to use item group codes to divide the test into two or more parts. For an odd-even split, go to the *Variables tab* and type the letter A for all of the even items and type the letter B for the odd items. After providing these item group codes, run the item analysis. A new table appears in the output, and it is labeled "Item Group Defined Part-Test Reliability." In this table are internal consistency estimates using the part-test scores. That is, all of the even items (group A) are summed to create a half-test score, and all of the odd items (group B) are summed to create another half-test score. These half-test scores are then used in the internal consistency estimates instead of item scores. Coefficient alpha in this table will be the same as the Spearman-Brown

RELIABILITY IF ITEM DELETED					
Item	L2	Alpha	F-G	F-B	Raju
item1	0.9169	0.9154	0.9169	0.9171	0.9154
item2	0.9150	0.9136	0.9150	0.9151	0.9136
item3	0.9171	0.9158	0.9171	0.9172	0.9158
item4	0.9159	0.9144	0.9159	0.9160	0.9144
item5	0.9159	0.9144	0.9159	0.9161	0.9144
item6	0.9167	0.9152	0.9167	0.9168	0.9152
item7	0.9148	0.9134	0.9148	0.9150	0.9134
item8	0.9170	0.9157	0.9170	0.9171	0.9157
item9	0.9152	0.9138	0.9152	0.9154	0.9138
item10	0.9156	0.9141	0.9156	0.9157	0.9141
item11	0.9155	0.9140	0.9155	0.9156	0.9140
item12	0.9165	0.9150	0.9165	0.9167	0.9150
item13	0.9147	0.9133	0.9147	0.9149	0.9133
item14	0.9161	0.9146	0.9161	0.9163	0.9146
item15	0.9167	0.9153	0.9167	0.9169	0.9153
item16	0.9156	0.9140	0.9156	0.9157	0.9140
item17	0.9165	0.9150	0.9165	0.9167	0.9150
item18	0.9175	0.9164	0.9174	0.9176	0.9164
item19	0.9160	0.9145	0.9160	0.9162	0.9145
item20	0.9140	0.9126	0.9140	0.9142	0.9126

FIGURE 5.5 Reliability if Item Deleted output

result when items have the same variances. Otherwise, the values will be slightly different. For example, coefficient alpha for the odd/even part-test reliability is 0.9216, which is very close the Spearman-Brown result of 0.9218.

You can also use the group codes to divide the test into more than two parts. It is up to you to choose how you would like to divide it. One possibility for a mixed format test is to place the binary items on one part and polytomous items on another. Partitioning the test in this manner allows you to evaluate the influence of item type on reliability (Qualls, 1995). If you have a test that contains testlets, another choice is to have each testlet represent a part (Feldt, 2002). It is up to you to choose which, if any, partitioning of the test into item groups, but jMetrik makes it easy for you to obtain part-test reliability estimates.

Be sure to remove the item group codes after you complete a reliability analysis. Rasch measurement procedures (described later) also use the item group codes but in a different way. To avoid the accidental use of group codes when you do not intend to use them, remove them from the *Variables tab* at the completion of the reliability analysis.

6

DIFFERENTIAL ITEM FUNCTIONING

Differential item functioning (DIF) occurs when one group of examinees has a different expected item score than comparable examinees from another group. It indicates that an item is measuring something beyond the intended construct and is contributing to construct irrelevant variance. It also suggests that the item is biased and unfair for some examinees. DIF is a threat to validity that should be identified and eliminated to improve the quality of inferences about the measured trait.

A DIF analysis compares the performance of two different groups of examinees. The focal group is the one of interest, and it usually represents a minority group such as black students or English language learners. Their performance is compared to a reference group that represents a larger group of examinees such as white students or native English speakers. A population of examinees may contain multiple focal and references groups, but a single DIF analysis involves only one pair of groups (e.g. Asian and white examinees). The analysis is repeated with different pairs of groups to evaluate DIF for a variety of focal and references groups.

One way to evaluate the performance of focal and reference group members is to compute the difference in mean item scores. This difference is referred to as item impact (Clauser & Mazor, 1998; Holland & Thayer, 1988), and it reveals a difference between the two groups, but it does not indicate a problem with the item. Item impact could be due to group differences on the measured trait. DIF is a distinct concept from item impact. DIF procedures control for group differences on the measured trait by evaluating the performance of comparable focal and reference group members. Differences in item performance for comparable focal and reference group members indicate a problem with the item that warrants further review.

Figure 6.1 illustrates DIF using two item characteristic curves. The curve on the left describes the probability of a correct response for male examinees, and the curve on the right shows the probability of a correct response for female examinees. DIF is indicated in this graph because for a given value of the measured trait (x-axis), males have a higher probability of a correct response (y-axis) than females. For example, at a value of Theta = 0, females have about a 25% chance of a correct response, whereas males have about a 72% chance of a correct response. Moreover, males have a greater probability of a correct response at all other values of the measured trait. This consistent advantage for one group is referred to as uniform DIF.

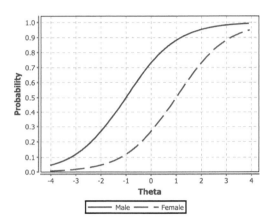

FIGURE 6.1 Plot of uniform DIF

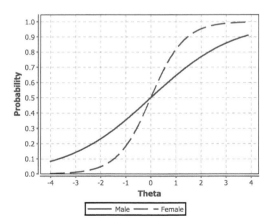

FIGURE 6.2 Plot of nonuniform DIF

Figure 6.2 shows a second type of DIF. In this figure, the probability of a correct response is greater for females at low parts of the scale (i.e. Theta < 0), but at higher parts of the scale, the probability is greater for males. This type of DIF is referred to as nonuniform DIF because one group has the advantage at one part of the scale, and the other group has the advantage at another part.

DIF is a threat to validity because it occurs when an item is measuring something beyond the intended trait, such as group membership. It is problematic in and of itself, but it does not automatically qualify as item bias. DIF only rises to the level of item bias if reviewers identify item content, language, or stereotypes that unfairly influence scores. Hambleton and Rodgers (1995) explain the way these item features can lead to item bias. Item content contributes to item bias when it is more familiar to members of one demographic group than another. For example, a writing composition question that asks students to write about a superhero will likely be easier for boys than girls even if they have the same writing ability. Reference to a superhero adds a gender-specific context to the item that is irrelevant to the measured trait. In a similar way, language produces bias when a word is interpreted differently by one demographic group than another. For example, a question written in English that uses a word with a similar sound but a different meaning than a Spanish word (i.e. a false cognate) can cause English language learners to perform worse than their native English counterparts. This differential performance might not be a matter of item bias if the false cognate appeared on an English test, but it would be a source of bias on a math test. Finally, offensive language or the depiction of stereotyped roles in an item can also contribute to bias. The offensive language will not make the item more difficult, but offended examinees may skip the question or fail to put forth effort in answering it. Reviewers check items for content, language, and stereotypes that warrant a claim of item bias, but they do not check every item. They only review items that exhibit DIF.

Procedures for identifying DIF involve a combination of statistical and practical significance. jMetrik provides the Cochran-Mantel-Haenszel (CMH) statistic for testing statistical significance, and it uses the common-odds ratio, ETS delta statistic, and the standardized mean difference (SMD) to describe practical significance. Statistical and practical significance combine to form three levels of DIF classification. The next three sections of the chapter describe methods for evaluating statistical significance, practical significance, and classification rules for describing the magnitude of DIF.

CMH Chi-Square Statistic

The CMH (Cochran, 1954; Mantel, 1963) procedure tests the null hypothesis that item scores are conditionally independent of group membership. It works by stratifying examinees on a matching score and evaluating the difference between the observed and expected item scores pooled over all strata. If this difference is unlikely to occur by chance, the null hypothesis is rejected. jMetrik uses the CMH test to provide a common method of analysis for binary and polytomous items. For binary items, this procedure reduces to the more familiar Mantel-Haenszel test of association in stratified 2×2 tables, albeit without the correction for continuity (see Holland & Thayer, 1988). The CMH has an acceptable type I error rate in long tests (e.g. 20 or more items) and adequate power to detect uniform DIF (Ankenmann, Witt, & Dunbar, 1999; Uttaro & Millsap, 1994). On the other hand, it has an inflated type I error rate with short tests, tests with varying item difficulty and discrimination, or tests in which the focal and reference group have a notably different average ability level (Ankenmann et al., 1999; Uttaro & Millsap, 1994). It also has difficulty detecting nonuniform DIF (Rogers & Swaminathan, 1990; Uttaro & Millsap, 1994).

The CMH statistic is computed from a contingency table arranged in the following way. Data for an item with $t = 1, \ldots, T$ score levels are organized into $k = 1, \ldots, K$ strata with each stratum having its own $2 \times T$ contingency table. The strata represent levels of the matching score. Table 6.1 shows the organization of data for the kth stratum.

The CMH statistic is given by

$$
CMH = \frac{\left(\sum_{k=1}^{K} F_k - \sum_{k=1}^{K} M_k \right)^2}{\sum_{k=1}^{K} Var(F_k)} \, ,
$$

where the sum of scores for the focal group is $F_K = \sum_{t=1}^{T} y_t n_{2tk}$. Under the null hypothesis, the expected value of F_k is

$$
M_k = \frac{n_{2+k}}{n_{++k}} \sum_{t=1}^{T} y_t n_{+tk} \, ,
$$

TABLE 6.1 $2 \times T$ contingency table for the kth stratum

Group	Item Score					Total
	y_1	y_2	y_3	$\cdots$	y_T	
Reference	n_{11k}	n_{12k}	n_{13k}	$\cdots$	n_{1Tk}	n_{1+k}
Focal	n_{21k}	n_{22k}	n_{23k}	$\cdots$	n_{2Tk}	n_{2+k}
Total	n_{+1k}	n_{+2k}	n_{+3k}	$\cdots$	n_{+Tk}	n_{++k}

and the variance of F_k is

$$Var(F_k) = \frac{n_{1+k}n_{2+k}}{n_{++k}^2(n_{++k}-1)}\left\{\left(n_{++k}\sum_{t=1}^{T}y_t^2 n_{+tk}\right)-\left(\sum_{t=1}^{T}y_t n_{+tk}\right)^2\right\}.$$

Note that a table is excluded from the computation if $Var(F_k)=0$. This can occur when a table includes a single examinee or when focal and reference group examinees respond to a binary question the same way.

Under the null hypothesis, the CMH statistic has a chi-square distribution with 1 degree of freedom. With a significance level of 0.05, the null hypothesis is rejected if CMH is 3.84 or larger.

Matching Score Considerations

Stratifying examinees on the matching score is a feature of the CMH procedure that distinguishes it from an item impact analysis. The purity of the matching score and number of strata have an effect on the efficacy of the CMH procedure for detecting DIF. One way to create a matching score is to compute a sum score using all items on the test. This score is easy to compute, but it can diminish the quality of matching if it includes items with DIF. Holland and Thayer (1988) recommend a two-step approach to purifying the matching score. In the first step, you conduct a DIF analysis with all items included in the sum score. You then compute a purified sum score from the non-DIF items identified in the preliminary analysis. In the second step, you conduct the final DIF analysis using the purified matching score. Items identified with DIF in the second step are flagged for review and possibly excluded from the test.

Purification improves the quality of matching by eliminating the influence of items with DIF, but it does not prevent problems that arise from having too few or too many score levels. Matching reference and focal group members at each level of the sum score is referred to as thin matching. It provides the most precision in matching and the greatest control over the measured trait. However, it can lead to the inadvertent exclusion of examinees from the analysis and a reduction in statistical power (Clauser & Mazor, 1998). This problem can be overcome by thick matching examinees with wider score levels (e.g. 0 to 5, 6 to 10). Thick matching preserves more of the available data and improves power, but it comes at the expense of less control over the measured trait. Indeed, thick matching with a single score level is nothing more than an item impact analysis.

Given the trade-offs with thick and thin matching, Donoghue and Allen (1993) identified conditions that were best for thin matching and those that were best for thick matching. They found that with a long test and a large sample size, thin matching worked best. They also found that thick matching worked better than thin matching with short tests and that some types of thick matching were better than others. One effective thick matching approach involved equal score intervals (e.g. 0 to 5, 6 to 10), and another involved score groups with equal percentages of examinees (e.g. quintile or decile score groups). In choosing the number of score levels for matching, you must consider test length and sample size and choose a matching score that optimizes the precision of matching and statistical power.

DIF Effect Sizes

The CMH procedure tests for statistical significance, and like other hypothesis tests, it is influenced by sample size. Therefore, it is necessary to incorporate practical significance into the identification of DIF. jMetrik uses three different effect sizes to quantify practical significance. For binary items, the effect size is the common odds ratio. It is computed by

$$\hat{\alpha}_{MH} = \frac{\sum_{k=1}^{K} n_{12k} n_{21k} / n_{++k}}{\sum_{k=1}^{K} n_{11k} n_{22k} / n_{++k}}.$$

This effect size ranges between 0 and infinity with a value of 1 indicating no DIF. Values of the common odds ratio larger than 1 indicate an item that favors the reference group, and values less than 1 indicate an item that favors the focal group.

Holland and Thayer (1988) proposed a transformation of the common odds ratio that results in a symmetric statistic. It is referred to as the ETS delta statistic in jMetrik, and it is given by $\Delta_{MH} = -2.35\ln(\hat{\alpha}_{MH})$. Negative values indicate an item that favors the reference group, and positive values signal an item that favors the focal group. No DIF is present when the ETS delta statistic is 0.

For polytomous items, jMetrik uses the SMD as the measure of effect size (Dorans & Schmitt, 1991). Zwick and Thayer (1996) describe the SMD as

$$SMD = \sum_{k=1}^{K} \frac{n_{2+k}}{n_{2++}} \left(\frac{F_k}{n_{2+k}} \right) - \sum_{k=1}^{K} \frac{n_{2+k}}{n_{2++}} \left(\frac{R_k}{n_{1+k}} \right),$$

where n_{2++} is the total number of focal examinees responding to the item and $R_K = \sum_{t=1}^{T} \gamma_t n_{1tk}$. For binary items, the SMD reduces to the standardized P-DIF (sP-DIF) statistic of Dorans, Schmitt, and Bleistein (1992).

ETS DIF Classification Levels

Zwick and Ercikan (1989) described ETS rules for classifying the magnitude of DIF. Stated in terms of the common odds ratio, these rules are as follows:

- "A" items have (a) a CMH p-value greater than 0.05, or (b) the common odds ratio is strictly between 0.65 and 1.53.
- "B" items are neither "A" nor "C" items.
- "C" items have (a) a common odds ratio less than 0.53, and the upper bound of the 95% confidence interval for the common odds ratio is less than 0.65, or (b) a common odds ratio greater than 1.89 and the lower bound of the 95% confidence interval is greater than 1.53.

A plus sign is added to the "B" and "C" classification to indicate an item that favors the focal group, and a minus sign is added to the classification to represent an item that favors the reference group. In simple terms, "A" items exhibit a negligible amount of DIF. They are good items with respect to DIF, and they should be retained in the test. "B" items show a moderate amount of DIF. These items should be reviewed for bias and revised or replaced with an alternative item. On the other hand, "C" items have large amounts of DIF and are of concern. In most cases, they should be eliminated from a test. The only reason to include a "C" item is if its elimination leads to a problem with content validity that is more severe than the problem caused by DIF.

Polytomous items have a similar classification scheme, but it only involves a consideration of practical significance. The rules follow the recommendations for the sP-DIF statistic by dividing the SMD by the item score range. This change to the SMD limits it to values between 0 and 1. Refer to this new value of the SMD as sP-DIF. According to (Dorans et al., 1992), the rules are as follows:

- "AA" items have an sP-DIF value strictly less than 0.05.
- "BB" items are neither "AA" nor "CC" items.
- "CC" items have an sP-DIF statistic that is 0.10 or larger.

As with the binary item classification levels, a plus sign is added to B and C items to indicate an item that favors the focal group. A minus sign is added to signal an item that favors the reference group.

Missing Data

Missing data can occur in a DIF analysis when an examinee has no group code, no value for the matching score, or no item response. Treatment of missing data differs depending on which variable is missing data. An examinee with no group code will be excluded from every DIF analysis that involves that group. For example, a

DIF analysis that compares the performance of males and females on 10 test items will omit an examinee that does not have a gender code (e.g. male or female). Moreover, this omission will occur for the analysis of all 10 items. An examinee with no matching score will similarly be omitted from every DIF analysis that uses that matching score. Finally, an examinee with a missing item response can be included or excluded from the analysis. The particular treatment of a missing item response depends on the option you select when running the analysis. The CMH and effect size statistics only involve examinees that are not excluded from the analysis.

Running the Analysis in jMetrik

You must create a matching score prior to running the DIF analysis in jMetrik. Use the test scaling feature (see chapter 3) to compute a sum score. You can use this variable as the matching variable, or you can convert it to decile scores with the ranking procedures in jMetrik. Once you have created a matching variable, start the *Cochran-Mantel-Haenszel DIF dialog* by clicking **Analyze → DIF: Mantel-Haenszel** (see Figure 6.3). The top part of the dialog shows a selection panel that is more elaborate than other selection panels that you have seen thus far. On the left side of the selection panel, it includes a list of all variables in the database. Select test items from this list, and click the first *Select button* to move your selection to the selected variable list. The dialog will only allow you to add items to this list. You can choose a single item for the analysis or multiple items. Once you have selected the test items, choose the variable that represents the matching score,

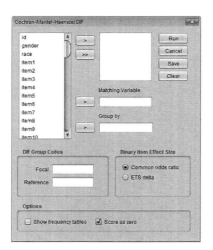

FIGURE 6.3 Cochran–Mantel–Haenszel DIF dialog

and press the *Select button* next to the *Matching Variable text field*. You can only add a numeric variable to the *Matching Variable text field*. Finally, click the variable that contains group identifiers, and press the last *Select button* next to the *Group by text field*. Your grouping variable can be text or numeric data.

After you have completed your selections, you must tell jMetrik about your focal and reference groups. Type the code representing focal group members in the *Focal text field* of the *DIF Group Codes panel*. Now, type the code for the reference group in the *Reference text field*. Nonnumeric focal and reference group codes are case sensitive. Be sure that your codes match the case of the grouping variable's data. For example, suppose your grouping variable is gender and the data are recorded as "F" and "M" for female and male, respectively. If you type "f" and "m" as the focal and reference group codes, you will not get the correct results. jMetrik will display "NaN" in the output because it will not have identified any members of the focal or reference group. Upper- and lowercase letters are viewed as different characters in jMetrik.

The remaining options in the dialog affect the effect size, treatment of missing item responses, and the display of output from the analysis. jMetrik uses the common odds ratio as the default effect size for binary items. You can change this to the ETS delta statistic by clicking the *ETS delta radio button* in the *Binary Item Effect Size panel*. The effect size is displayed in the output along with other information from the analysis. If you would like to add frequency tables to the output, select the *Show frequency tables checkbox* in the *Options panel*. This option will substantially increase the amount of output. You will see a contingency table for every level of the matching score and every item. For example, an analysis with 60 items and a sum score matching variable will add in $60 \times 61 = 3,660$ tables to the output. You should only select the *Show frequency tables checkbox* if you have reason to explore the data in more detail. Finally, jMetrik will score missing item responses as 0 points if the *Score as zero checkbox* is selected. If you unselect this option, examinees with a missing item response will be excluded from the analysis of that item.

Example 1: Binary Items

The first example uses the exam1 data. This table already includes a variable for the sum score, but if has been deleted, you can create another sum score variable using the test scaling feature in jMetrik. To avoid loss of data due to thin matching, create decile scores using the *Rank Values dialog*. Click **Transform → Ranking** to start the dialog. Select the sum score, type "deciles" as the new variable name, and choose the *Deciles option* from the drop-down menu. Click the *Run button* to execute the analysis and create the new variable.

Start the *Cochran-Mantel-Haenszel DIF dialog* by clicking **Analyze → DIF: Mantel-Haenszel**. Select all test items in the first list of the selection panel.

Choose `deciles` as your matching variable, and select `gender` as the grouping variable. Use the focal code "F" (without quotes) for female examinees and the reference code "M" (without quotes) for male examinees. Be sure you type uppercase letters. The codes are stored in the data as uppercase letters. Therefore, the codes you type in the dialog should be uppercase. Use the default options for the binary item effect size and output display. Click the *Run button* to run the analysis.

Figure 6.4 displays the output for the first 10 items. In order of appearance, the columns shown in this output contain the (a) item name, (b) CMH chi-square statistic, (c) p-value for the CMH statistic, (d) valid sample size, (e) effect size and 95% confidence interval for the effect size in parentheses, and (f) ETS DIF classification. Two of these columns need additional explanation. As explained earlier, thin matching can lead to sparse tables and the exclusion of some examinees from the calculation of the CMH statistic. The valid sample size column shows the number of examinees included in the CMH chi-square statistic and effect size calculation. Following this column is the column labeled "E.S. (95% C. I.)." It contains an effect size for each item, but it does not indicate which effect size is listed. For binary items, it will list either the common odds ratio or ETS delta statistic. The particular value displayed depends on the option you selected in the *Binary Item Effect Size panel* of the dialog. For polytomous items, this column lists the SMD statistic. You must be aware of the item type when interpreting the effect size because the effect size for binary items is different from the effect size for polytomous items.

Of the items shown in Figure 6.4, `item6` has the largest chi-square statistic at 19.95 ($p < 0.01$). The commons odds ratio for this item is 0.74, which indicates that the item is almost one and a half times ($1/0.74 = 1.41$) easier for reference group examinees. `Item4` appears to be the best item in Figure 6.4. It has a chi-square value of 1.81 ($p = 0.18$) and a common odds ratio of 1.08. This item is neither statistically nor practically significant for DIF. Although the complete output is not shown, a total of 28 items have a statistically significant chi-square statistic at the 0.05 level. However, the effect sizes are all negligible resulting in a classification of A for all exam1 items when evaluating DIF for males and females. This finding underscores the importance of considering statistical and practical significance. Exam1 includes responses from 6,000 examinees, which leads to

Item	Chi-square	p-value	Valid N	E.S. (95% C.I.)			Class
item1	9.61	0.00	5687	0.82 (	0.73,	0.93)	A
item2	1.78	0.18	5687	1.08 (	0.97,	1.20)	A
item3	2.94	0.09	5687	1.14 (	0.98,	1.33)	A
item4	1.81	0.18	5687	1.08 (	0.97,	1.21)	A
item5	11.92	0.00	5687	0.81 (	0.72,	0.91)	A
item6	19.95	0.00	5687	0.74 (	0.65,	0.85)	A
item7	2.88	0.09	5687	1.10 (	0.98,	1.23)	A
item8	14.02	0.00	5687	1.39 (	1.17,	1.66)	A
item9	4.25	0.04	5687	0.89 (	0.79,	0.99)	A
item10	6.12	0.01	5687	1.22 (	1.04,	1.44)	A

FIGURE 6.4 DIF results for exam1 data

many items showing statistical significance. In terms of practical significance, no items ever reach the threshold for B or C items.

Although exam1 appears to be free of DIF for males and females, let's evaluate DIF for different race groups. Run a second DIF analysis using the race variable to compare black (focal code = B) and white examinees (focal code = W). Use the same decile score for the matching variable. Results show that item45 is a B+ item with a chi-square value of 73.6 (p < 0.01) and a common odds ratio of 0.54. This item favors the focal group but still warrants further review. The more problematic item is item37. It too favors the focal group with a chi-square value of 99.89 (p < 0.01) and a common odds ratio of 0.49. This magnitude of DIF is large and qualifies as a C+ item. This item should be reviewed and replaced with a better item. The remaining items are all A items.

To determine if the large amount of DIF in item37 has influenced the quality of matching, conduct a second analysis with a purified matching score. First, compute a sum score without item37. Then, compute purified decile scores. When you run the analysis with the purified decile score, you will see that item37 remains a C+ item, but item45 becomes worse with a classification of C+. This result justifies the decision to review both items and find better items to take their place.

Example 1 highlights a challenge often encountered in DIF analysis. An item may appear free of DIF when comparing one pair of groups but not another pair. This result raises the question of whether the item should be retained or excluded from the test. Perhaps the best approach is to review an item that shows DIF for any comparison. The decision to remove it or not really depends on whether DIF qualifies as item bias, the balance of test content with and without the item, and whether a suitable replacements exist for the item.

Example 2: Mixed Format Test

The second example uses the dif-sim1 data that can be found in the dif folder of the example data files. These data include responses for 1,500 examinees to 50 binary items and 2 four-category polytomous items. There are 1,000 reference group members and 500 focal group examinees in the file. Reference and focal group codes are listed in the group variable.

Descriptive statistics for each group can be computed by first creating two subsets of data—one for the focal group (group = 1) and another for the reference group (group = 0). Reference group scores have a mean of 30.22 and a standard deviation of 12.98. By comparison, the focal group scores are about half a standard deviation lower with a mean of 23.36 and a standard deviation of 13.1.

Start the *Cochran-Mantel-Haenszel DIF dialog* and select all items for the analysis and choose sumscore as the matching variable. Next, click the *Save button* to start the *New Table Name dialog*. Type a name for the output table in that dialog. Type the focal and reference group codes, but use the default options for the binary item effect size and the frequency tables. Click the *Run button* to execute the analysis. Figure 6.5 lists the results for the first 15 items. Item5, item10, and item15 show a large amount of DIF that favors the reference group. The common odds ratio for these 3 items ranges from 3.52 to 4.79, which indicates that reference group members are between four and five times more likely to answer these items correctly than focal group examinees. At the opposite end of the spectrum, item30 and item40 are C items that favor the focal group. The common odds ratio for item30 indicates that focal group examinees are 6.25 (i.e. $1/0.16 = 6.25$) times more likely to answer the item correctly than reference group examinees. Similarly, focal group members are 6.25 times more likely to answer item40 correctly.

To quickly summarize the ETS Classification levels for all items, select the output table produced from the analysis, and compute frequencies for the etsclass variable. A large majority of the items (42) are A or AA items. Three items are B+ items and suggest a moderate amount of DIF. The remaining 7 items show a large amount of DIF with 2 favoring the focal group (i.e. 2 C+ items) and 5 favoring the reference group (i.e. 5 C– items).

The large number of B and C items is concerning, and it could affect the quality of matching and the final results. Therefore, you should purify the matching score by creating a sum score that only involves the A and B items. Use the test scaling feature to create a sum score without any of the C items, and call this new variable pure_sumscore. Run the DIF analysis again. Select all of the items for the analysis, but use pure_sumscore as the matching variable.

Results from the second analysis reveal that 45 items are A items, and 7 items are C items (see Figure 6.6). Notice that there are no longer any B items in the results. This result is correct because the data were simulated to have a large amount of DIF in item5, item10, item15, item20, item30, item40, and item52 and no DIF in the remaining items. Thus, there should be no B items in these data. The B items from the first analysis were an artifact of using a nonpurified matching score. We correctly identified the DIF items by purifying the matching score and running the analysis a second time.

Item	Chi-square	p-value	Valid N	E.S. (95% C.I.)			Class
item1	1.21	0.27	931	1.24 (	0.84,	1.83)	A
item2	1.54	0.21	1252	0.82 (	0.59,	1.12)	A
item3	8.65	0.00	1293	0.66 (	0.50,	0.88)	A
item4	0.03	0.87	1376	0.98 (	0.74,	1.29)	A
item5	75.07	0.00	1301	3.52 (	2.62,	4.72)	C–
item6	0.01	0.91	1086	1.02 (	0.72,	1.45)	A
item7	0.18	0.67	779	0.90 (	0.56,	1.46)	A
item8	0.03	0.87	1194	0.97 (	0.66,	1.41)	A
item9	2.91	0.09	1004	0.68 (	0.44,	1.06)	A
item10	124.19	0.00	1306	4.79 (	3.57,	6.42)	C–
item11	0.19	0.66	1193	1.07 (	0.78,	1.48)	A
item12	8.33	0.00	1103	0.62 (	0.44,	0.86)	B+
item13	3.66	0.06	1376	0.76 (	0.57,	1.01)	A
item14	3.12	0.08	1060	0.73 (	0.52,	1.03)	A
item15	90.35	0.00	1248	4.66 (	3.34,	6.52)	C–

FIGURE 6.5 DIF results for a mixed format test

Item	Chi-square	p-value	Valid N	E.S. (95% C.I.)			Class
item1	4.15	0.04	1017	1.49 (	1.02,	2.19)	A
item2	0.23	0.64	1267	0.93 (	0.68,	1.27)	A
item3	4.91	0.03	1341	0.73 (	0.55,	0.97)	A
item4	1.03	0.31	1418	1.16 (	0.88,	1.52)	A
item5	95.40	0.00	1406	3.99 (	2.99,	5.33)	C-
item6	1.28	0.26	1263	1.22 (	0.86,	1.71)	A
item7	0.16	0.69	745	1.10 (	0.69,	1.77)	A
item8	0.35	0.56	1175	1.12 (	0.77,	1.63)	A
item9	1.83	0.18	998	0.73 (	0.47,	1.14)	A
item10	136.13	0.00	1328	5.06 (	3.79,	6.76)	C-
item11	1.29	0.26	1198	1.20 (	0.87,	1.65)	A
item12	2.11	0.15	1230	0.78 (	0.57,	1.09)	A
item13	1.15	0.28	1382	0.86 (	0.65,	1.13)	A
item14	0.71	0.40	1116	0.86 (	0.61,	1.21)	A
item15	111.75	0.00	1276	5.29 (	3.80,	7.37)	C-

FIGURE 6.6 DIF results using a purified matching score

Even though some items favor the reference group and others favor the focal group, the conservative decision is to remove all C items from the test and replace them with better items.

7

RASCH MEASUREMENT

The item analysis and reliability methods discussed in chapters 4 and 5 are primarily based on classical test theory methods. They are easy to implement and understand, but they suffer from a number of limitations. In particular, classical test theory methods are population dependent. Item statistics and reliability estimates are influenced by the group of examinees, and examinee scores are influenced by the characteristics of the items included on an exam. Item difficulty, discrimination, and test score reliability can change substantially when computed from data obtained from different populations. For example, gifted examinees will tend to answer an item correctly more often than examinees from the general population. Consequently, item difficulty estimates will be higher (i.e. easier) for the population of gifted students than it will be for the general population. There will also be less heterogeneity in gifted populations resulting in lower reliability estimates than those obtained from the general population. The primary way of dealing with the influence of the population on item and test characteristics in classical methods is to make sure that the entire population is represented in the sample and that it is represented in the right proportions. However, this practice only solves one side of the problem.

Examinee performance depends on the difficulty of the test items in the classical approach to testing. Test scores will be lower if examinees are administered difficult items, but scores will be higher if examinees are assigned easy items. In a similar fashion, reliability will be high when a group of examinees takes a test with moderately discriminating items, and it will be low if the same group of examinees takes a test composed of items with extreme discrimination values.

The problem with the dependency between population and item characteristics can be highlighted with a sports analogy. Imagine that a group of athletes are competing in the high jump and that the height of the bar is measured in feet instead of meters. However, suppose further that the definition of a "foot" is the length of an athlete's right foot. Setting the bar at "three feet" will result in a lower bar for an athlete with smaller feet than it will for an athlete with larger feet. Therefore, tall athletes with small feet would perform the best in this type of high jump. Those with large feet would be at a disadvantage because the bar will be set higher than it would be for athletes with small feet. The only way to break this dependency is to use a measure of height that is not related to the length of an athlete's foot. Similarly, we need a measurement model that produces item statistics that are independent of the examinee population, and we need to estimate examinee ability independently of item characteristics. Item response theory provides the solution to this problem. In this chapter, we focus on one item response model in particular—the Rasch model.

The Rasch Model

To motivate the development of the Rasch model, consider a continuum of values that represent the construct of interest. Low levels of this continuum represent characteristics of the latent trait that frequently occur or are easily observed. Conversely, high levels of this continuum indicate characteristics that are more rarely observed or that are more difficult to achieve. A person's standing on the latent trait[1] is denoted by θ, and it represents how far along the continuum that we expect the person to answer items correctly. The examinee will correctly answer all items below this point but incorrectly answer all items above this point. Also on this continuum are values of item difficulty, which represent how far along the continuum that we expect to obtain correct responses to the item. Item difficulty is denoted with the letter b. With both the person and item represented on this continuum, we would like to see a person answer an item correctly every time $\theta \geq b$ and incorrectly otherwise. However, this relationship is deterministic and does not account for other possibilities during a test. It is possible for examinees with low values of θ to answer a difficult item correctly, and it is also possible for examinees with high values of θ to make a mistake and answer an easy item incorrectly. The Rasch model uses a logistic function to represent the probability that a randomly selected examinee with ability level θ correctly answers an item. The model for a response from examinee i to item j is given by

$$P_{ij}(\theta) = \frac{\exp(\theta_i - b_j)}{1 + \exp(\theta_i - b_j)}.$$

The probability of a correct response, $P(\theta)$, increases monotonically as the value of the latent trait increases.[2] In the Rasch model, this probability has a lower asymptote of 0 and an upper asymptote of 1. If item difficulty is larger than person ability (i.e. $\theta < b$), the examinee is unlikely to answer the item correctly. If an examinee's value of the latent trait is the same as item difficulty ($\theta = b$), then the examinee has a 50% chance of answering the item correctly. As the value of the latent trait exceeds item difficulty (i.e. $\theta > b$), the probability of a correct response increases beyond 50%.

Figure 7.1 illustrates an item characteristic curve for the Rasch model (chapter 9 describes procedures for creating this plot). Person ability is on the x-axis of this figure, and the probability of a correct response is on the y-axis. Item difficulty is also referred to as the location parameter because it affects how far the curve is shifted left or right along the x-axis. Low difficulty values shift the entire curve to the left, and high difficulty values shift the whole curve to the right. That is, small values of item difficulty represent easy items because moving the curve to the left increase the probability of a correct response at a given level of ability. Conversely, large values of item difficulty represent difficult items because moving the curve to the right lowers the probability of a correct response for a given level of ability. This interpretation of difficulty is opposite that of item difficulty in a classical item analysis, but it is in the more intuitive direction—small values are easy items, and large values are difficult items.

A benefit of item response theory is that person and item parameters are on the same scale. That is why we can use a single continuum to represent the standing of a person and an item. In the Rasch model, parameters are on a logit scale. A logit is the log-odds of a correct response, and it represents the distance between the person and item. Specifically, the logit is $\log\{P(\theta)/[1-P(\theta)]\} = \theta - b$.

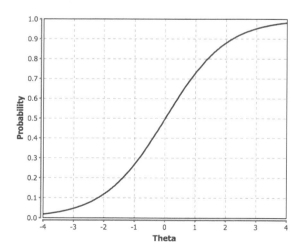

FIGURE 7.1 Rasch model item characteristic curve

This result gets back to the original motivation of describing the interaction between a person and an item. If the person's value of the latent trait exceeds item difficulty, then the person is likely to get the item correct. Otherwise, the person is likely to get it incorrect.

The Rasch model and many other item response models make two assumptions: (a) the test measures a single latent trait (i.e. it is unidimensional), and (b) items are locally independent. The first assumption means that we assume to measure one and only one latent trait. There are item response models that allow for multidimensional latent traits, but they are not discussed here. The assumption of local independence means that once you control for the latent trait, items are unrelated to each other. That is, at a given level of ability, a response to one item is not influenced by any other item. You should evaluate both of these assumptions anytime you use the Rasch model analysis in jMetrik because there are some test design characteristics that may violate these assumptions. For example, a math test that requires a substantial amount of reading may violate the assumption of unidimensionality because students need reading and math skills to obtain high scores. If a student lacks the needed reading skills, his scores on the math test will be reduced as compared to someone with the same math ability but with adequate reading skills. The assumption of local independence may be similarly violated because of test design. For example, a test composed of testlets may violate local independence. A testlet is like a test within a test and it results from designing a test in which items share a common stimulus. An example of a testlet is a reading test with multiple sequences of a reading passage followed by several questions about the passage. Responses to items for one passage tend to be more related to items from different passages. If severe enough, testlets can violate the assumption of local independence. Violation of either of these assumptions can affect the estimation of model parameters.

Parameter Invariance

A primary benefit of item response theory is that item and person parameters are invariant. Item parameters do not depend on the distribution of examinees, and person parameters do not depend on the distribution of items (Lord, 1980). Parameter invariance means that we can change the person ability distribution without affecting the item characteristic curve. With respect to the distribution of items, it means that we can change the distribution of items on a test without affecting examinee ability. Parameter invariance is a reason why computer adaptive testing works; we get the same estimate (within measurement error), albeit more efficiently, with tests that are tailored to each individual examinee. Parameter invariance solves the problem of population dependence that exists in classical test theory. Returning to our sports analogy, parameter invariance means that the height of the bar is no longer measured in units specific to each athlete's foot. Height is measured independently of every athlete with a metric ruler.

Although parameter invariance is an attractive property of item response theory, it only holds for the population parameters, not the estimates of those parameters. There are two common ways that a lack of invariance can occur. Differential item functioning (DIF) indicates a lack of invariance between the reference and focal group. It indicates that the item characteristic curve would be notably different for the reference and focal groups. The second way to observe a lack of invariance is item parameter drift, a type of DIF that occurs in the context of test linking and equating. Invariance only holds for the estimates if the item response model perfectly fits the data. Therefore, we must test for a lack of invariance and evaluate model fit before assuming that invariance holds for our estimates. Methods for detecting DIF and drift are discussed in other chapters. Those methods are relevant to the current chapter because of their implications about parameter invariance.

Specific Objectivity

Parameter invariance applies to all item response models, not just the Rasch model. However, the Rasch model boasts additional measurement properties related to comparisons between persons and comparisons between items. Specific objectivity (Rasch, 1977) is a principle of invariant comparisons that is realized by the Rasch family of item response models. With respect to item response models, specific objectivity implies that the difference between two examinees is independent of the items and that the difference between two items is independent of the examinees. Specific objectivity concerns the comparison of items or comparison of persons, not just individual item or person parameters. In this way, it differs from parameter invariance and is a distinguishing characteristic of the Rasch family of models.

Embretson and Reise (2000) clearly explain invariant person comparisons and invariant item comparisons implied by specific objectivity. Given two examinees with ability parameters θ_1 and θ_2 and an arbitrary item with difficulty b_j, compute the difference in logits for these two examinees by $(\theta_1 - b_j) - (\theta_2 - b_j)$. With a little algebra, this difference becomes $\theta_1 - \theta_2$, a quantity that does not depend on the item difficulty parameter. Thus, the difference between these two examinees will be the same for any item. Invariant item comparisons can be demonstrated in a similar way.

To show that specific objectivity is unique to the Rasch family of models, consider the logit for a two-parameter logistic model, $a_j(\theta - b_j)$. This model includes an additional parameter, a_j, that represents the slope of the item characteristic curve at the point of inflection. Consequently, the difference between two examinee ability parameters depends on item discrimination, $a_j(\theta_1 - b_j) - a_j(\theta_2 - b_j) = a_j(\theta_1 - \theta_2)$. That is, the comparison of persons changes with each item; specific objectivity does not hold in item response models that allow items to have different discrimination parameters. The same result can be demonstrated for the comparison of two items for these models.

Indeterminacy of the Latent Scale

Rupp and Zumbo (2006) note that parameter invariance and specific objectivity pertain to parameters that are on the same scale. However, the latent scale in the Rasch model and all other item response models is completely arbitrary. This problem is referred to as scale indeterminacy, and it means that parameters are unique only up to a linear transformation (de Ayala, 2009). If you add a value to item difficulty and add the same value to person ability, the probability of a response does not change. Any linear transformation of the parameters results in the same probabilities. For the Rasch model, the indeterminacy is in the origin. The unit of measurement in the Rasch model is fixed to 1. In item response models that involve a discrimination parameter, indeterminacy applies to both the origin and unit of measurement. Scale indeterminacy must be resolved prior to estimation of any parameters. In the Rasch model, indeterminacy is resolved through either person centering or item centering (de Ayala, 2009). jMetrik uses the item-centering approach by default. It does this by constraining item difficulty to have an average value of 0. Once model constraints that resolve scale indeterminacy are established, parameters of the models can be estimated.

Parameter Estimation

jMetrik uses joint maximum likelihood (JML) to estimate parameters for the Rasch, partial credit, and rating scale models. The algorithm begins with initial values computed by the normal approximation (PROX) procedure (Wright & Masters, 1982) and then iteratively updates item difficulty parameters and updates person ability parameters in an alternating fashion. It continues to switch back and forth between item updates and person updates until the largest change in logits is smaller than the convergence criterion (0.005 by default). jMetrik uses a proportional curve-fitting algorithm to update item and person parameter estimates instead of the Newton-Raphson procedure described by Wright and Masters. This method is more stable than the Newton-Raphson procedure, particularly with polytomous item response models and small sample sizes (Linacre, 2012). Meyer and Hailey (2012) provide complete details of the JML algorithm in jMetrik and describe its efficacy in recovering model parameters.

Item and Person Fit

Like parameter invariance, specific objectivity only holds for our estimates when the model perfectly fits the data. Although perfect model fit is unlikely in practice, we can design tests that fit good enough to assume parameter invariance and specific objectivity hold. Infit and outfit are two types of statistics commonly encountered in Rasch measurement that can be computed to check for item and person fit. Infit and outfit statistics begin with the difference between the observed and expected values of an item response, a difference known as a residual, $y_{ij} = X_{ij} - P_{ij}(\theta)$. There are as many residuals as there are actual item responses in the data file. Residuals are then standardized by dividing them by their item information. To compute outfit for an item, standardized residuals are squared and averaged over examinees. To calculate outfit for a single examinee, standardized residuals are squared and averaged over items. Outfit gives disproportionate weight to person–item encounters that involve an extreme mismatch between the item and person (e.g. low ability examinee responding to a difficult item). As such, it is "sensitive to unexpected responses made by persons for whom [the item] is far too easy or far too difficult" (Wright & Masters, 1982, p. 99). It is referred to as outfit because of its sensitivity to these outliers. To adjust for this limitation of outfit, Wright and Masters provided a weighted average of squared standardized residuals, where the weights are the item information. This statistic is referred to as infit because it is information weighted, thereby emphasizing residuals from well-matched person–item encounters (e.g. person ability similar to item difficulty), and places less emphasis on residuals from mismatched person–item encounters.

Infit and outfit mean square residual fit statistics have an expected value of 1 and are always positive in value. Values close to 1 indicate good model–data fit, and values diverge from 1 as the degree of misfit increases. Bond and Fox (2007) explain that values greater than 1 signal underfit because the data contain more variation than expected by the Rasch model. Item responses tend to be the opposite of what we expect from the model. For example, an infit or outfit value of 1.25 indicates that the data have 25% more variance than expected by the model. Underfitting items indicate a problem with our measure and should be reviewed for appropriateness. They should not be removed on the basis of misfit alone, but on substantive grounds through consideration of item content and the measured construct. If an underfitting item is deemed to measure something other than the target construct or noted to measure it in an unusual way, it should be removed from the test.

Infit and outfit mean square fit statistics less than 1 are also of concern, but these values indicate a different type of problem. They reflect a tendency for responses to be too consistent with what we expect from the model. Extremely small infit and outfit values indicate that item responses are completely determined by the model. As a result, our measure will appear to have a better quality than it actually does (Bond & Fox, 2007). The extent to which the data have less variance than expected by our model is reflected in the statistic. For example, an outfit statistic of 0.6 indicates that the data have 40% less variance than expected by the model.

There are different rules of thumb for deciding whether an item or person fits well. They are synthesized here to provide you with guidance. A narrow range of infit and outfit mean square values such as 0.8 to 1.2 is recommended for high-stakes tests (Bond & Fox, 2007), but values between 0.5 and 1.5 are still productive for measurement (Linacre, 2012). Of most concern are infit and outfit mean square values larger than 2.0 because they degrade the measure. Less concerning are small infit and outfit values, but the quality of the measure will be artificially inflated with values smaller than 0.5 (Linacre, 2012). Keep in mind that these are rules of thumb and should not be used reflexively. They should serve as flags for items or persons that need extra attention.

Thus far, the discussion has focused on mean square fit statistics, but there are also standardized infit and outfit statistics that may be of interest. Standardized infit and outfit values are t-statistics that take on positive and negative values and have an expected value of 0. Items or persons with standardized infit and outfit values greater than 3 in absolute value indicate a problem with fit and warrant additional scrutiny. Note that standardized infit and outfit statistics are sensitive to sample size. As such, they are only useful for sample sizes less than 300 examinees (Linacre, 2012).

Classical item analysis and Rasch measurement procedures are often combined in practice to identify good items for a test. In this spirit, Linacre (2012) provides the following recommendations for practice: (a) identify items with negative item-total correlations (i.e. negative classical item discrimination), (b) evaluate outfit before infit, (c) examine mean square fit statistics before standardized fit statistics, and (d) focus on high values before low values. His recommendations highlight the strength of both approaches to test design. Item selection procedures in classical test theory tend to focus on item discrimination, whereas item selection procedures in Rasch measurement emphasize item and person fit.

In jMetrik output from a Rasch model analysis, the two outfit statistics are labeled *UMS* and *Std. UMS* to indicate the unweighted mean square fit statistic and standardized unweighted mean square fit statistic, respectively. Likewise, the two infit statistics are labeled *WMS* and *Std. WMS* in jMetrik output to indicate the weighted mean square fit statistic and standardized weighted mean square fit statistic, respectively.

Scale Quality Statistics

Reliability and separation are two scale quality statistics in Rasch measurement that can be computed for either items or persons. Person reliability represents the quality of person ordering on the latent trait. It is similar to the reliability coefficient in classical test theory. It is computed as the ratio of true person variance on the latent trait to observed variance on the latent trait. True person variance on the latent trait is computed by subtracting mean square measurement error from the variance of latent trait estimate for the sample of examinees (see Wright & Masters, 1982). Person reliability will be larger for heterogeneous samples than it will be for samples in which everyone has a similar value of the latent trait. It will also be larger with longer tests than it will be with shorter tests because the latent trait values will be estimated more precisely. As with classical test theory, person reliability values larger than 0.8 are desirable, but this rule of thumb must be balanced with a consideration of the heterogeneity of the sample and purpose of testing.

Person separation is similar to reliability in that it represents the extent to which a measure can reproduce and consistently rank scores. It is a signal-to-noise ratio computed by dividing the true person variance on the latent trait by the root mean square measurement error. Separation values larger than 2 are desirable. Person separation indicates the standard deviation of latent trait values in standard error units (Wright & Masters, 1982). Typically, person separation and reliability are used in conjunction to evaluate the quality of a measure.

Item reliability and separation are computed similarly, but the interpretation is different. Item reliability refers to how well item difficulties can be rank ordered. It is affected by the spread of item difficulty values and the sample size. Linacre (2012) notes that low item reliability can occur when the sample size is too small to obtain stable item difficulty estimates. Item separation provides similar information about the quality of locating the items on the latent trait. Ideally, item separation values should be larger than 2.

Running the Analysis in jMetrik

To run the analysis, click **Analyze → Rasch Models (JMLE)** to display the *Rasch Models dialog*. The upper part of the dialog allows you to select binary and polytomous items for the analysis in the same way you would select them for an item analysis. The lower portion of the dialog includes three different tabs that provide (a) global options, (b) item options, and (c) person options. Each tab is explained below.

Global Options

Figure 7.2 shows a screenshot of the *Global tab*.

The parts of this tab are the (a) *Global Estimation panel*, (b) *Missing Data panel*, and (c) *Linear Transformation panel*. Two of the options listed on the *Global Estimation panel* pertain to the JML algorithm. *Max iterations* refers to the maximum number of iterations in the JML algorithm. It is the maximum number of times that the algorithm will switch between updating item parameters and updating person parameters. The default value is 150, which should be adequate for most data sets. JML iterations will continue until the algorithm reaches the value

FIGURE 7.2 Global Options tab

specified in the *Max iterations text field* or until the maximum change in logits is less than or equal to the value specified in the *Convergence criterion text field* of the *Global Estimation panel*. The default convergence criterion is 0.005. After you run a Rasch model analysis in jMetrik, the number of iterations and the maximum change in logits at each iteration is listed in the log. It is a good practice to check this information after each analysis to ensure that the algorithm converged and did not reach the maximum number of iterations. If you did reach the maximum number of iterations before satisfying the convergence criterion, run the analysis again using a larger value for max iterations. Run the analysis for as many iterations as necessary to reach the convergence criterion. In most cases, the convergence criterion can be reached in a few iterations.

You have two options for handling missing data in a Rasch model analysis. The default option is to ignore missing data by selecting the *Ignore radio button* in the *Missing Data panel*. When this option is selected, item and person parameter estimates are based on the available data. It is common to use this option when there is planned missing data such as data from a computer based test or data that combine responses from multiple test forms. It is also common to ignore missing data when the analysis is aimed at obtaining item parameter estimates for item banking. In other situations, ignoring missing data may not be appropriate. For example, an omitted response for an item from a traditional paper-and-pencil test may be due to a lack of knowledge on the examinee's part. Consequently, it may make more sense to score this type of missing response as incorrect when producing an estimate of examinee ability. In such a case, select the *Score as zero radio button* option in the *Missing Data panel* to have missing data scored as 0 points. Keep in mind that your choice for handling missing data will affect the estimation of person and item parameters.

Testing programs often use two runs of the data. The first run is aimed at obtaining item parameter estimates, not person ability estimates, and missing data is ignored. The second run focuses on estimating person ability parameters by fixing item parameter values at their values from the first run or values stored in an item bank. Missing data are scored as incorrect during the second run to estimate examinee ability.

The *Linear Transformation panel* allows you to specify a transformation of the logit scale for the person and item parameter estimates. This transformation is applied at the conclusion of the estimation algorithm. It is not applied between iterations. All person and item parameters will be transformed to have a mean and standard deviation (i.e. intercept and scale) that correspond to the values you provide in this panel. For example, suppose you would like estimated person parameters to have a mean of 50 and a standard deviation of 10 (i.e. a T-score). Enter 50 in the *Mean text field* and 10 in the *Scale text field* to apply this transformation.

The transformation is conducted by first estimating the mean and standard deviation of the parameters of interest (e.g. person ability or item difficulty), which is denoted as X. It then uses the transformation $X^\star = AX + B$, where the scale transformation coefficients are $A = \sigma/S$ and $B = \mu - A\overline{X}$. In these equations, σ is the scale value you provided, and S is the standard deviation of the current parameter estimates. Likewise, μ is the value you provided for mean in the *Linear Transformation panel*, and $\overline{X}$ is the mean of the current parameter estimates.

As an alternative to the transformation panel, you can use **Transform → Linear Transformation** on person or item parameter estimates that you save to a table. A benefit of that alternative is additional control over the transformation. See the chapter on test scaling for more information about this procedure.

Finally, the *Precision text field* in the *Linear Transformation panel* refers to the number of decimal places retained for item and person parameters after the transformation is applied. The default precision is 4. As such, only four decimal places will be retained after the transformation. If you wish to use a different number of decimal places, type that number in the *Precision text field*.

Item Options

Figure 7.3 shows a screenshot for the *Item tab*. The parts of this tab are the (a) *Item Options panel* and the (b) *Item Estimation panel*. The *Item Options panel* includes three options.

Choose the *Correct UCON bias checkbox* to multiply item difficulty values by a factor of $(n - 1)/n$, where n is the number of items in the analysis. This correction is applied to item difficulty, threshold, and person ability values at the end of the estimation algorithm, and it adjusts item difficulties to correct for bias due to the use of JML estimation. Choose the *Show start values checkbox* if you would like to add PROX start values to the output file. The last option on the *Item Options panel* allows you to save parameter estimates to a new database table. Select the *Save item estimates checkbox*, and type a name for the new table in the corresponding text field to create a table of estimates and fit statistics.

FIGURE 7.3 Item Options tab

In practical applications of item response theory, you may want to fix item parameter estimates to existing values produced during a previous run or obtained from an item bank. The *Item Estimation panel* is where you select items from an item parameter table (see the appendix) for which you would like to fix the estimates to existing values. Click the *Select button* to display a new dialog that contains three lists (dialog not shown). The first list on the left side of the dialog contains all of the database tables. You must select an item parameter table in this list to continue. If you do not select an item parameter table, you will see an error message. When you select a table in this list, the variables contained in the table will be displayed in the second list. Click variables in this list and move them to the third list to fix item difficulty to the values in the item parameter table. Note that items are matched by name when fixing values. That is, an item name in the item parameter table must match an item name in the data table being analyzed. Only successful matches will result in fixed parameter values.

Person Options

Figure 7.4 shows a screenshot for the *Person tab*. The parts of this tab are the (a) *Person Options panel* and the (b) *Person Estimation panel*. Options in the *Person Estimation panel* are not currently active, but they will be available in a future release of jMetrik.

Three options in the *Person Options panel* give you control over the information saved to the database. Choosing the *Save person estimates checkbox* will add five new variables to the item response table. New variables are the sum score (`sum`), valid sum score (`vsum`), latent trait estimate (`theta`), standard error for the latent trait estimate (`stderr`), and an indicator of whether the examinee had an extreme score (`extreme`). Sum is the sum of points earned from all items, and valid sum score is the sum of item scores for items completed by an examinee. As described previously, latent trait estimates will be affected by your choice of handling missing data. The default method is to ignore missing data, but you may want to change this to score as 0 when producing person ability estimates.

FIGURE 7.4 Person Options tab

When you select the *Save person fit statistics checkbox*, jMetrik will add four new variables to the item response table. The new variables are for the weighted mean squares (`wms`), standardized weighted mean squares (`stdwms`), unweighted mean squares (`ums`), and standardized unweighted mean squares (`stdums`) fit statistics. jMetrik will use unique item names each time the person estimate and fit statistic variables are added to the table. It does this by adding a number to the end of each variable. For example, if you run the analysis twice with the option to save person estimates, the person ability values will be stored in a variable called `theta` from the first analysis and `theta1` for the second analysis. The number added to the end of the variable name represents the order in which the variables were created.

Finally, the *Save residuals checkbox* will produce a new table that contains residual values when selected. The number of rows in this table will be the same as the number of rows in the original item response table, and the number of columns will be the number of items included in the analysis. When you select the *Save residuals checkbox*, a text field will become active, and you can type a name for the new table in that text field. Use this new table to check the assumption of local independence using Yen's Q_3 statistic (Yen, 1984). The next chapter describes this statistic in more detail and provides an example of it.

Example 1: Multiple-Choice Items

Example 1 is an analysis of the exam1 data using the default options and the additional option of saving item statistics to a new table. jMetrik provides three tables in the text output that provide information from the analysis. Figure 7.5 shows a portion of the Final JMLE Item Statistics output table. The first column of this table lists the item name, the second column lists the item difficulty estimate, and the third column contains the standard error of the difficulty estimate. Subsequent columns in the table provide infit and outfit statistics. The columns labeled WMS and Std. WMS are the weighted mean square and standardized infit statistics, respectively. These are followed by the columns labeled UMS and Std. UMS, which provide the unweighted mean square and standardized outfit statistics, respectively.

Among the items shown in Figure 7.5, item8 is the easiest with a difficulty value of −1.86, and item7 is the most difficult with a difficulty estimate of 0.47. According to the mean square fit statistics, no items show signs of degrading the measure. None of the items in Figure 7.5 show signs of underfitting, but a couple of items (e.g. item3 and item10) show a slight tendency to overfit the data. Notice that several of the standardized infit and outfit statistics appear to be very large. These extreme values are mostly due to the large sample size ($N = 6,000$) and are not indicative of poor fit. Focus on the mean square fit statistics whenever you have a large sample size. It is a good idea to review fit statistics and difficulty estimates for every item in the output, but it is also possible to get a quick look at the distribution of these statistics for the entire test.

A benefit of having produced a new table of item statistics is that you can run descriptive statistics and graphs on the results to quickly summarize the analysis. To compute descriptive statistics, click **Analyze → Descriptives**, and select the variables of interest (e.g. bparam, wms, and ums). Among all 56 items, difficulty ranges from a low of −1.8589 to a high of 2.21. Of course, the average difficulty is 0, given the way indeterminacy is resolved in the Rasch model. Mean square outfit statistics range from 0.6414 to 1.4538 and have an average value of 0.9926. The minimum and maximum values are outside the desired range for a high-stakes test and indicate that some items may need additional scrutiny. No items are flagged as problematic with respect to mean square infit statistics. These values range from 0.8057 to 1.1748 and have a mean of 0.9962.

A careful review of outfit for each item reveals that item27 is the most problematic with a UMS value of 1.4538. It is not surprising that this item is also the most difficult on the test. A similar pattern is evident for item32, which has the second largest UMS value and second largest item difficulty. For these two items, difficulty may be so high that even very capable examinees tend to resort to guessing. Or, it could be that the correct answer is ambiguous. Some evidence of this latter hypothesis is taken from the classical item analysis. Both item27 and item32 were flagged as problematic in the classical item analysis because

			FINAL JMLE ITEM STATISTICS			
Item	Difficulty	Std. Error	WMS	Std. WMS	UMS	Std. UMS
item1	−0.80	0.03	1.03	1.81	1.01	0.24
item2	0.13	0.03	1.12	10.42	1.14	8.98
item3	−1.48	0.04	0.88	−5.92	0.75	−7.31
item4	−0.09	0.03	1.13	11.77	1.19	11.22
item5	−0.50	0.03	1.05	4.32	1.10	4.87
item6	−0.94	0.03	0.98	−1.39	0.96	−1.60
item7	0.47	0.03	1.05	4.61	1.08	5.22
item8	−1.86	0.04	0.86	−5.62	0.64	−8.88
item9	0.04	0.03	1.05	4.88	1.06	3.60

FIGURE 7.5 Item difficulty and fit statistics for exam1 data

of positive distractor-total correlations. Thus, there is enough evidence that these items deserve additional attention. Item review techniques such as expert review or examine think-aloud procedures could provide insight as to whether there is indeed any problem with these items.

The opposite pattern is evident with item8 and item11. Item8 is the easiest item and the one with the lowest UMS values. Item11 has the second lowest difficulty estimate and second lowest UMS statistic. Neither of the outfit statistics are of concern, but they do suggest that easy items have a tendency for overfitting the data.

Figure 7.6 shows a portion of the Score Table from the Rasch model output. In the Rasch model, the sum score is a sufficient statistic for the examinee ability estimate. The one-to-one correspondence between the sum score and examinee ability value is shown in the Score Table. The first column in the Score Table lists the sum score, and the second column lists the corresponding value of examinee ability. For example, a sum score of 3 points has a corresponding ability value of −3.13, and a score of 10 has an ability value of −1.7. Although scores of 0 and the maximum possible sum score are listed in the Score Table, these values are considered to be extreme values. They are not estimated during the JML algorithm, but in a separate run that is only conducted for extreme persons and items. Finally, the third column in the Score Table lists the standard error of ability estimate. Notice that the standard error is not homogenous across ability levels. It is a conditional standard error with larger values for ability values at the extreme and smaller values for ability values near the middle.

To produce ability estimates for every examinee, you must select the *Save person estimates checkbox* in the *Person tab* of the *Rasch Models dialog*. Saving ability estimates for every examinee is necessary for score reporting. It also helps you summarize the distribution of examinee ability estimates. Using all items from the exam1 data, examinee ability estimates range from −3.3057 to 5.5013 with a mean of 0.3042 and a standard deviation of 0.9974. The distribution of examinees is slightly above the distribution of items, a relationship we will explore in more detail with an item map in a later chapter.

SCORE TABLE		
Score	Theta	Std. Err
0.00	−5.52	1.83
1.00	−4.29	1.02
2.00	−3.57	0.73
3.00	−3.13	0.60
4.00	−2.81	0.53
5.00	−2.55	0.48
6.00	−2.34	0.45
7.00	−2.15	0.42
8.00	−1.99	0.40
9.00	−1.83	0.38
10.00	−1.70	0.36
11.00	−1.57	0.35

FIGURE 7.6 Score table for exam1

```
SCALE QUALITY STATISTICS
==============================================
Statistic                 Items      Persons
----------------------------------------------
Observed Variance         0.5696     0.9870
Observed Std. Dev.        0.7547     0.9935
Mean Square Error         0.0009     0.1062
Root MSE                  0.0304     0.3258
Adjusted Variance         0.5687     0.8809
Adjusted Std. Dev.        0.7541     0.9385
Separation Index         24.7988     2.8805
Number of Strata         33.3984     4.1739
Reliability               0.9984     0.8924
==============================================
```

FIGURE 7.7 Scale quality statistics for exam1

If you also saved person fit statistic to the data table, you will see that mean square infit ranges from 0.0101 to 1.5328 and mean square outfit statistics range from 0.0054 to 3.3019. If you would like to quickly identify the misfitting exam-inees, you can subset the data to show only those examinees with WMS and UMS values that exceed your criterion. For example, select the data table that contains the person fit statistics, click **Manage → Subset Cases**, and then type wms < 0.5 OR wms > 2.0 OR ums < 0.5 OR ums > 2.0 in the text area. Type a name for the new table, and click the *OK button*. You will get a new table of 22 examinees with infit and outfit values outside the specified range. You can then look further into why these examinees are displaying misfit. Note that you could also do the opposite and subset the data to include only those examinees that show good fit.

Finally, the last table in the Rasch model output is labeled Scale Quality Sta-tistics. Figure 7.7 shows this table for the exam1 data using all items and persons for the analysis. Person reliability is 0.8924, a value that is very similar to the value of coefficient alpha (0.9106) reported in chapter 6. The corresponding person separation index is about 2.88 indicating that our measure is able to adequately rank order people on the latent trait. On the item side, reliability and separation are very large indicating that the sample is large enough to consistently rank order items by difficulty.

This chapter focused on the Rasch model for binary items. The next chapter expands on the Rasch family of models and describes two models for polytomous items.

Notes

1 In educational measurement, people often refer to θ as *person ability* or *examinee proficiency* because it relates to an examinee's capability to correctly answer items in a particular content domain. However, *latent trait* is a more general term that refers to examinee characteristics in a cognitive domain such as math ability or examinee characteristics in a psychological domain such as motivation, attitude, or well-being that are not directly observable. These terms are used interchangeably throughout this book.
2 Subscripts for examinee ability and item difficulty will be dropped whenever possible to simplify the presentation.

8

POLYTOMOUS RASCH MODELS

The Rasch model presented in the last chapter is suitable for items scored as right or wrong, such as multiple-choice and true-false questions. It is not suitable for polytomous scored items, such as Likert scales. Masters's (1982) partial credit model and Andrich's (1978) rating scale model are two extensions of the Rasch model that are appropriate for polytomous items. Choosing a polytomous item response model depends on the testing context and procedures for item scoring. In educational settings, students may be awarded points that represent different degrees of correctness. For example, students taking a math test may be given no points for a completely incorrect answer, partial credit (1 point) for correctly answering part of the problem, and full credit (2 points) for correctly solving the whole problem. Students may also complete tasks that award credit for particular characteristics of a response. For example, students may be asked to write a short essay that is scored in one of five possible score levels (e.g. 0, 1, 2, 3, 4) that represent progressively more sophisticated qualities of creative writing.

A rating scale item is another type of polytomous scored item that is commonly encountered in psychology and education. A Likert scale item is an example. This type of item has a stem (e.g. I am happy today) to which the examinee responds by selecting one response from a set of ordered possibilities: "Strongly Agree," "Agree," "Disagree," or "Strongly Disagree." Rating scale items differ from a partial credit item in two important ways. First, there is no correct answer. Any response provided by the examinee is appropriate, and it reflects the extent to which an attitude or attribute is endorsed by the examinee. Second, rating scale items typically use the same response options for every item, whereas partial credit items use different scoring criteria for each item. These differences between partial credit and rating scale items give rise to different item response models.

Masters's partial credit model is appropriate when each item has its own scoring criteria. Andrich's rating scale model is designed for Likert items and other items that share the same scoring criteria.

Polytomous Item Response Models

Masters's partial credit model (1982) is an extension of the Rasch model for items that use partial credit scoring. It describes the probability of an examinee obtaining one of the possible item scores. For an item j with $h = 1, \ldots, m_j$ response categories, the probability of the response k is given by

$$P_{jk}(\theta) = \frac{\exp \sum_{v=1}^{k} (\theta - b_j - \tau_{jv})}{\sum_{h=1}^{m_j} \exp \sum_{v=1}^{h} (\theta - b_j - \tau_{jv})},$$

where θ, b_j, and τ_{jv} are the person ability, item difficulty, and category threshold parameters, respectively. Person ability has the same interpretation as it did in the Rasch model, and item difficulty still refers to the overall location of the item. The threshold parameter is new. It represents the point where the responses for the kth and $k+1$th categories are equally likely, relative to item difficulty. For an item with m_j ordinal categories, there are only $m_j - 1$ threshold parameters. To eliminate indeterminacy in the model, item difficulty is constrained to have an average value of 0 across items, and threshold parameters are constrained to sum to 0 within an item.

jMetrik uses a version of the partial credit model that decomposes the step parameter into an overall item difficulty parameter, b_j, and a category threshold parameter, τ_{jv}. The subscript j on the threshold parameter indicates that each item has its own set of thresholds. Adding the item difficulty and a threshold parameter results in the step parameter, $b_{jv} = b_j + \tau_{jv}$, which indicates the point on the latent scale where two adjacent score categories intersect. A threshold parameter also represents the point where two adjacent score categories intersect, but the point is relative to item difficulty.

Andrich's (1978) rating scale model is a special case of the partial credit model such that all items that comprise the rating scale are constrained to have the same threshold parameters. The model is given by

$$P_{jk}(\theta) = \frac{\exp \sum_{v=1}^{k} (\theta - b_j - \tau_{v})}{\sum_{h=1}^{m_j} \exp \sum_{v=1}^{h} (\theta - b_j - \tau_{v})}.$$

The only difference between this equation and the one for the partial credit model is the missing item subscript, j, on the threshold parameter. Specifically, the step parameter for the rating scale model is $b_{jv} = b_j + \tau_v$, which differs only by a subscript from the step parameter for the partial credit model, $b_{jv} = b_j + \tau_{jv}$. This missing subscript indicates that the same threshold parameters apply to all items that make up the rating scale. A common set of thresholds is suitable for items that share the same response options, such as Likert scales. Thus, the rating scale model is often applied in psychological research that uses such item formats.

Another reason for using the rating scale model in lieu of the partial credit model is to reduce the number of parameters and improve estimation of the thresholds. If you run an analysis by treating all items as partial credit items and the set of estimated thresholds is similar across items, then you have reason to combine the items into a single rating scale and estimate a single set of thresholds. Standard errors for the threshold parameters will become smaller because of the additional information obtained from multiple items during the estimation process.

The meaning of the step and threshold parameters in the partial credit and rating scale models is best explained in a graph. Figure 8.1 shows option characteristic curves for a partial credit item with four categories. In this figure, there are three places where the curves for two adjacent categories intersect. The first intersection occurs at an ability level of about −1.7. This value is the step parameter for transitioning from a score of 0 to a score of 1. The next intersection point is at about 0.8, and it represents the point where the probability of scoring in category 1 is the same as scoring in category 2. The remaining step parameter is located at

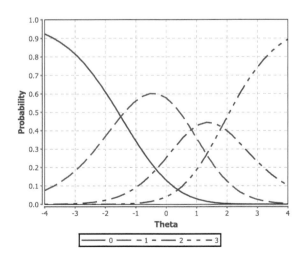

FIGURE 8.1 Option characteristic curves with widely spaced step parameters

about 1.8 on the latent scale. Beyond this level of ability, examinees are most likely to obtain the highest possible item score.

There are two aspects to consider when evaluating threshold parameters for a polytomous item response model. The first is the spread of threshold estimates. A nice feature of the item graphed in Figure 8.1 is that the step parameters range from about −1.7 to +1.8. A consequence of this spread of step parameters is that the item will provide information throughout most of the scale's range. It contrasts with a polytomous item that focuses information on a more concise range of scores because of a narrow range of step values. Figure 8.2 illustrates a partial credit item with a narrow range of step parameters. Notice that the intersection points are all between −0.8 and +0.8.

It is up to you to decide whether a narrow or wide range of step parameters is desirable. The choice depends on whether you would like information spread across a wide range of the scale as in a norm-referenced test, or if you would like information focused on a more specific point along the latent scale. Neither a narrow nor a wide spread of step parameter indicates a problem, but one type may be preferred given the purpose of your measure. There are other arrangements of step parameters that are indicative of a problem.

The second feature to consider is whether the thresholds are reversed. Reversals are one arrangement of step parameters that should concern you. A reversal occurs when a lower category is more difficult to endorse than a higher category. Figure 8.3 illustrates a reversal. Notice that the intersection of the category 0 and category 1 curves comes after (theta ≈ 0.3) the intersection of the category 0 and category 2 curves (theta ≈ 0.05). Because of this reversal, category 1 is never

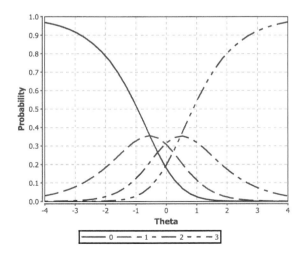

FIGURE 8.2 Options characteristic curves with narrowly spaced step parameters

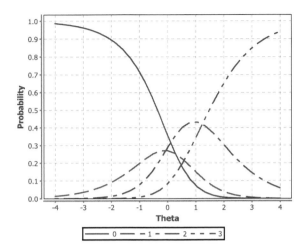

FIGURE 8.3 Options characteristic curves with a reversal

the most probable response. Ideally, a partial credit or rating scale item should have no reversals, and there should be some point along the latent scale where each response category is the most probable. If you find a reversal, you should take a closer look at the item and try to determine why the reversal is occurring. Does it indicate a problem with the scoring rubric? Does it mean that the score levels are not well defined or not distinct enough for raters to differentiate among responses? A reversal alone is not grounds for eliminating an item, but it does indicate that the item needs some attention. You may decide to refine the item and score levels after reviewing the item.

Note that this discussion of Figures 8.1 through 8.3 focused on the step parameters because the figures illustrate the actual positions of the curves on the latent scale. They do not illustrate the positions relative to item difficulty, which is the information conveyed in the threshold parameters. However, all of the comments about step parameters in this section also apply to the threshold parameters because the spacing between threshold values is the same as it is for the step parameters. The only difference is that the threshold parameters are relative to item difficulty and step parameters reflect the actual position on the scale. As such, plots based on threshold parameters would be centered about 0 in a graph and not shifted left or right by item difficulty as is the case for plots that use step parameters.

Category Fit Statistics

Fit statistics for the Rasch model described in the previous chapter are also applicable to the partial credit and rating scale models. In addition to these statistics, jMetrik provides category fit statistics that describe the fit of the model to specific categories. Category infit and outfit statistics use a category residual, which differs from the residual of an overall item response described in the previous chapter. The category residual describes the difference between the category value and the expected value of a person's response to the item, $y_{ijk} = k - E_{ij}(\theta)$. Category infit (WMS) uses an information-weighted average of the squared category residuals, whereas the category outfit statistic (UMS) uses an average of the squared category residuals. Although the category residuals differ from the overall item residuals, both infit and outfit statistics have the same interpretation for category fit as they do for overall item fit.

Running the Analysis in jMetrik

Steps for running an analysis with the partial credit or rating scale model are exactly the same as they were for the Rasch model. However, you need to provide additional information if you would like to use the rating scale model. jMetrik uses information from the *Variables tab* to automatically determine whether to apply a partial credit or rating scale model to a polytomous item. It will apply the partial credit model to any polytomous item that is not in any item group, and the rating scale model to any group with two or more items. That is, if there is no code in the *Group column* of the *Variables tab*, jMetrik will use the partial credit model for a polytomous item. If you type a letter or numeric code in the *Group column* for two or more items, then a rating scale model will be applied to all items that have the same code. Stated differently, the codes in the *Group column* of the *Variables tab* tell jMetrik how to group items into rating scales. You can create one or more item groups in any way you choose as long as each group has at least two items. jMetrik will apply the rating scale model to groups with two or more items. If a group has only one item or no group is specified in the *Variables tab*, jMetrik will use the partial credit model instead of the rating scale model.

It is also important to pay attention to item scoring when conducting a Rasch models analysis in jMetrik. Item scoring must always begin at 0. This requirement is true for binary and polytomous items. People have a tendency to start polytomous item scoring at 1, but you should resist this temptation and start the scoring at 0. It makes no difference whether you have multiple-choice, Likert scale, essay, short answer, or any other type of item scored in two or more categories. Item scoring must start at 0 for an analysis with any of the Rasch family of models in jMetrik.

Example 1: Mixed Format Test

Example 1 is an analysis of the exam3 data. Item1 through item20 in this data file are binary items, and the remaining five items are polytomous with scores ranging from 0 to 4. Although the score levels are the same for each polytomous item, we will use the partial credit model because the scoring criteria are different for each item. You should have already entered the scoring information into jMetrik so that it can distinguish between binary and polytomous items. To be sure that jMetrik uses the partial credit model for item21 through item25, check that no group codes are listed in the *Group column* of the *Variables tab*. jMetrik will identify binary and polytomous items and automatically select the correct model for each item type.

Figure 8.4 shows an excerpt of the Final JMLE Item Statistics table from the analysis. It contains the item difficulty estimates, standard errors, and overall item fit statistics as described in the previous chapter. Of the five items listed in Figure 8.4, item2 is the easiest with a difficulty value of −1.33, and item5 is the most difficult. Most of these items show adequate fit, but item2 shows signs of slight overfitting.

In the full output file (not shown), item8 is the easiest item (−1.47), and item5 is the most difficult (1.34). Infit statistics for all items range from 0.78 to 1.26, and outfit statistics range from 0.76 to 1.4. Item14 appears to have the worst fit with infit and outfit values of 1.26 and 1.4, respectively. All of the polytomous items have infit and outfit statistics less than 1. The largest amount of overfitting occurs with item21 with infit and outfit values of 0.78.

Anytime you run an analysis with polytomous items, a new table appears in the output. It is titled "Final JMLE Category Statistics," and it contains threshold parameter estimates, standard errors, and fit statistics for every partial credit item or rating scale item group. Figure 8.5 shows a portion of this table for the exam3 analysis. Each item in this table has the same number of threshold estimates, but the estimates are unique to each item. This result is due to the use of the partial credit model for each item.

Of the items displayed in Figure 8.5, item21 has the widest range of thresholds. They range from a low of −0.99 to a high of 1.22. Item23 has the next widest range of thresholds with values ranging from −1.2 to 0.95. However, item22 and item23 each have a reversal. Notice that with item22 the threshold for category 4 is easier than the threshold for category 2 and category 3. Scoring procedures (e.g. rubric score levels) for this item deserve attention because it is easier for examinees to obtain a score of 4 than a score of 2 or 3. It may be possible to rewrite the scoring criteria and eliminate the reversal. Item23 also

```
                        FINAL JMLE ITEM STATISTICS
============================================================================
Item        Difficulty   Std. Error    WMS     Std. WMS    UMS     Std. UMS
----------------------------------------------------------------------------
item1          0.58         0.10       0.96      -0.87     0.96      -0.53
item2         -1.33         0.11       0.87      -2.69     0.76      -3.12
item3         -0.77         0.10       0.90      -2.64     0.86      -2.52
item4         -0.60         0.10       1.03       0.92     1.01       0.16
item5          1.34         0.12       1.01       0.10     1.03       0.27
```

FIGURE 8.4 Item difficulty estimates and fit statistics for exam3

```
                    FINAL JMLE CATEGORY STATISTICS
==============================================================
Group           Category     Threshold     Std. Err      WMS        UMS
--------------------------------------------------------------
item21          0
                1            -0.99         0.13          0.72       0.65
                2            -0.49         0.11          0.75       0.76
                3             0.26         0.12          0.85       0.81
                4             1.22         0.16          0.77       0.84

item22          0
                1            -0.29         0.12          0.81       0.73
                2             0.05         0.12          0.82       0.70
                3             0.22         0.13          0.78       0.58
                4             0.02         0.14          0.89       0.83

item23          0
                1            -1.20         0.14          0.91       0.90
                2            -0.66         0.11          0.88       0.87
                3             0.95         0.13          1.04       1.10
                4             0.91         0.16          0.96       0.94
```

FIGURE 8.5 Category threshold estimates and fit statistics for exam3

shows a reversal, but it is not as serious as the one for item22. For item23, the estimated threshold for category 4 is smaller than the estimated threshold for category 3, but the difference in thresholds is small. Indeed, the standard errors are larger than the difference in thresholds. This reversal may disappear with a larger sample size and more precise estimates of the threshold parameters.

Regarding category fit statistics in Figure 8.5, all of the items show a tendency toward overfitting. None of the infit or outfit values are of concern, especially when considered along with the overall item fit statistics. The Rasch and partial credit models appear to fit these data well. There are some items that deserve additional attention and perhaps some revision, but nothing indicates a serious problem with fit.

As with an analysis that involves only Rasch model items, the output for analysis of a mixed format test also includes the score table and scale quality statistics table. These tables have the same meaning and interpretation as described in the previous chapter. For the exam3 data, person reliability is 0.86, and the separation index is 2.4. These values may be improved by adding items to the test. With only 25 items, it is a fairly short test.

As mentioned in the previous chapter, jMetrik includes an option for saving residuals to a new table. You can make use of this option to check the assumption of local independence with Yen's Q_3 statistic, which is defined as the correlation of residuals for a pair of items (Yen, 1984). If the latent trait accounts for all of the dependence among items, the residual correlation is expected to be 0. There is a slight negative bias to Yen's Q_3, but any value more extreme than ± 0.2 indicates a problem with local independence. If you find large values of Yen's Q_3, check the content of the items and try to determine the reason why the items are related. The items could have a shared stimulus or reflect individual steps in a multistep problem, or they could be items at the end of the test not reached by many examinees.

Using the option to save residuals, you can compute Yen's Q_3 by selecting the output table that contains the residuals and then running a correlation analysis on this table by clicking **Analyze** → **Correlation**. Select all of the items in this dialog, and click the *Run button* to produce a correlation matrix. There are numerous correlations in the correlation matrix, but you should take the time to look at all of the correlations below (or above) the diagonal. Make note of any values more extreme than ±0.2. For the exam3 data, no correlations are this extreme. The most extreme negative Q_3 statistic is −0.1769 for `item2` and `item11`, and the most extreme positive Q_3 statistic is 0.1457 for `item4` and `item5`. In terms of local independence, everything looks fine for exam3. You should get in the habit of checking local independence for every analysis that involves item response theory, not just those that use polytomous item response models. Every operational analysis should check the assumption of local independence, regardless of whether your analysis involves the Rasch, partial credit, or rating scale model.

Example 2: Likert Scale Items

This example will use the exam2 data to demonstrate the use of Andrich's rating scale model. As shown in the *Group column* of the *Variables tab* (see Figure 8.6), all of the items belong to group A, and the rating scale model will be applied to these items when you run the Rasch models analysis. Each item will have its own difficulty estimates and a common set of threshold parameter estimates.

Figure 8.7 shows a portion of the Final JMLE Item Statistics table for exam2. Of the items shown in this table, `item5` is the easiest (−1.06), and `item6` is the most difficult (0.61). All of these items appear to have good infit and outfit statistics. Among all of the items (details not shown), item difficulty ranges from −1.97 to 0.65. All of the items display good fit with infit values ranging from 0.83 to

Variable	Type	Scoring	Group
id	Not Item		
item1	Polytomous Item	(0,0,1,0,2,0,3,0) (0,0,1,0,2,0,3,0)	A
item2	Polytomous Item	(0,0,1,0,2,0,3,0) (0,0,1,0,2,0,3,0)	A
item3	Polytomous Item	(0,0,1,0,2,0,3,0) (0,0,1,0,2,0,3,0)	A
item4	Polytomous Item	(0,0,1,0,2,0,3,0) (0,0,1,0,2,0,3,0)	A
item5	Polytomous Item	(0,0,1,0,2,0,3,0) (0,0,1,0,2,0,3,0)	A
item6	Polytomous Item	(0,0,1,0,2,0,3,0) (0,0,1,0,2,0,3,0)	A

FIGURE 8.6 Item group codes in the Variables tab

```
                        FINAL JMLE ITEM STATISTICS
================================================================================
Item      Difficulty    Std. Error      WMS    Std. WMS      UMS     Std. UMS
--------------------------------------------------------------------------------
item1        -0.97         0.06         1.15       2.23      1.14       1.71
item2         0.17         0.05         1.14       2.38      1.07       1.08
item3         0.38         0.05         0.83      -3.16      0.92      -1.28
item4         0.47         0.06         0.99      -0.17      0.97      -0.44
item5        -1.06         0.06         1.07       1.13      1.05       0.58
item6         0.61         0.06         1.06       1.02      1.05       0.75
item7        -0.05         0.05         1.04       0.75      0.99      -0.09
```

FIGURE 8.7 Item difficulty estimates and fit statistics for exam2

FINAL JMLE CATEGORY STATISTICS					
Group	Category	Threshold	Std. Err	WMS	UMS
A	0				
	1	-0.81	0.03	0.99	1.00
	2	0.04	0.02	0.98	0.97
	3	0.76	0.03	1.00	0.99

FIGURE 8.8 Rating scale threshold estimates for exam2

1.15 and outfit values ranging from 0.77 to 1.14. For the entire scale, person reliability is 0.91, and the person separation index is 3.27. All of these statistics support the use of the rating scale model with these data.

Figure 8.8 shows the entire Final JMLE Category Statistics table from the analysis. Notice that it only contains a set of thresholds for group A even though there were 20 polytomous items on this test. Combining all of these items into a single group resulted in a single rating scale model for the entire group. That is, this set of thresholds applies to all 20 items. Instead of repeating these same values 20 times, the output lists them once for the entire group. Thresholds that range from a low of −0.81 to a high of 0.76, and there are no reversals. Although it seems that these thresholds do not cover much of the latent scale, these items actually span the latent scale from −2.78 to 1.41 when converted to step parameters by adding thresholds to item difficulty. The fit of these categories is good with all category infit and outfit values close to 1.

9

PLOTTING ITEM AND TEST CHARACTERISTICS

jMetrik provides two methods for plotting item and test characteristics. The first uses parameters from an item response model, and the second involves nonparametric methods to estimate item and test characteristics directly from the data. These methods provide additional tools for exploring item quality and selecting items for a test.

Characteristic Curves and Information Functions

As discussed in chapter 7, an item characteristic curve illustrates the relationship between the latent trait and the probability of a correct answer. It is a monotonic increasing function, which means that the probability of a correct answer increases as the latent trait increases. An examinee with a high level of ability has a greater chance of answering an item correctly as compared to an examinee with low ability. In addition to illustrating this relationship, it conveys information about item difficulty.

Item difficulty affects the location of an item characteristic curve. As item difficulty increases, the entire curve shifts to the right side of the plot. This feature is illustrated in Figure 9.1. Item A is the easiest of these three items with a difficulty of −1.0. Item B is more difficult and shifted to the right of Item A. It has a difficulty of 0. Item C is the most difficult of these three items and it is the rightmost curve in the plot. Item C has a difficulty of 1.0. Because item difficulty affects the location of the item characteristic curve, you can obtain the item difficulty parameter value directly from a plot of the item characteristic curve. For the Rasch model, difficulty is the point on the x-axis where the probability of a correct answer is 0.5. You can find item difficulty from a plot such as Figure 9.1

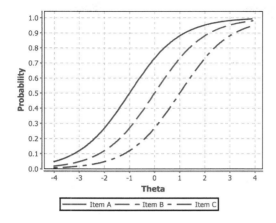

Theta

Item A ——— Item B — — Item C

FIGURE 9.1 Item characteristic curves for three Rasch model items

by drawing a horizontal line from the value 0.5 on the y-axis until it reaches an item characteristic curve. Then, draw a vertical line down to the x-axis to obtain the difficulty value.

Item difficulty for the partial credit and rating scale models also influences the overall location of the characteristic curves. As difficulty increases, the entire set of curves shifts to the right. As it decreases, the curves move to the left. Characteristic curves for polytomous items are also influenced by the threshold parameters. These values indicate the point where curves for adjacent score categories intersect and describe the extent to which the score categories are ordered. If threshold parameters increase in value as the response category increases, then each response option will be the most likely response for some range of examinee ability. Figure 9.2 illustrates option characteristic curves for a four-category polytomous item. This item is of moderate difficulty as indicated by the central placement of the curves in the figure. It also shows that the score categories are properly ordered. Threshold parameters range from about −1.2 to 1.2, and they increase in value. Examinees with an ability value less than −1.2 are most likely to select option 0, and those with an ability value between −1.2 and 0.2 are most likely to choose option 1. Continuing up the scale, examinees with ability between 0.2 and 1.2 are most likely to select option 3, and those with an ability value greater than 1.2 are most likely to choose option 3. If threshold parameters do not increase in value with each score category, then the curves would exhibit a reversal. This occurrence is not necessarily a flaw with the item, but it provides reason to closely evaluate item content and scoring rules. Item and option characteristic curves allow you to focus on individual items, but they can be combined to provide an overall summary of a complete test.

A test characteristic curve (TCC) describes the regression of true scores on person ability, and it plays a central role in item response theory (IRT) scale linking and score equating as described in chapter 10. It is obtained by summing the $j = 1, \ldots, J$ item characteristic curves, $\tau(\theta) = \sum_{j=1}^{J} \sum_{k=1}^{m_j} k P_{jk}(\theta)$ where $P_{jk}(\theta)$ is the probability of responding in category k. Figure 9.3 shows the TCC for the difsim data.

Characteristic curves are useful tools for illustrating the relationship between the probability of a response and person ability, but there is another function

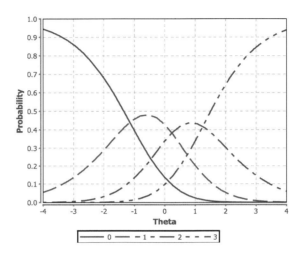

FIGURE 9.2 Option characteristic curves for a partial credit model item

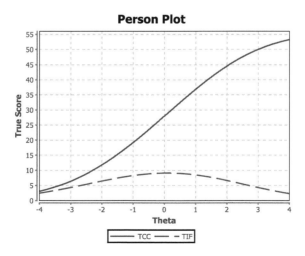

FIGURE 9.3 A test characteristic curve and test information function

that describes the quality of measurement more directly. The item information function, $I_j(\theta)$, describes an item's contribution to measurement of person ability such that the greater the amount of information, the more precision there is in estimating the person ability. Item information is neither a linear function nor uniform in nature. It is shaped like an anthill. As such, item information is large at one part of the scale and small at others. A Rasch model item contributes maximum information at ability values that equal item difficulty. This relationship is illustrated in Figure 9.4. The item in this figure has a difficulty of 0.04, and the information function reaches its peak when the ability level is 0.04. Thus, the item in Figure 9.4 provides the best measurement of people with an ability level of 0.04. It also provides useful information for examinees with ability between −1.0 and 1.0. Outside of this range, the item does not contribute much to measurement of the latent trait. Additional items are needed to improve measurement precision at other parts of the scale.

Item information functions combine in a simple way to summarize measurement precision for an entire test. Specifically, the test information function (TIF) is the sum of item information functions, $I(\theta) = \sum_{j=1}^{J} I_j(\theta)$. Figure 9.3 shows the TIF for the difsim data. It has a maximum near 0 and takes on reasonably large values between −1.5 and 1.5. As a result, examinees with ability level in this region will be measured more precisely than those outside of it.

Test information guides test development in IRT. It is used to design a test with maximal precision at important parts of the scale. An item from the Rasch family of models will contribute maximum information at the point where person ability equals item difficulty. As a result, if you need more information at a

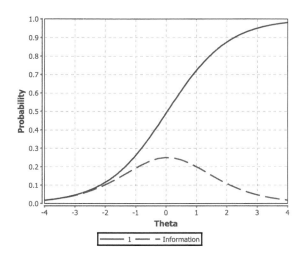

FIGURE 9.4 An item characteristic curve and item information function

particular point on the scale, then choose items with that level of difficulty. For example, if you would like to have a lot of measurement precision at an ability level of 1.2, then choose test items with a difficulty at or very near 1.2. This will result in a TIF that reaches its peak at 1.2. Maximizing information at an important region of the scale allows you to minimize measurement error in that region because of the relationship between information and measurement error. The standard error of the examinee ability estimate is inversely related to information, $SE(\theta) = 1 / \sqrt{I(\theta)}$. Small values of information translate to large standard errors, and large values of information result in small standard errors.

Item Maps

Item maps summarize the distribution of person ability and distribution of item difficulty or step parameters for an entire test. They are useful for determining whether items align with the examinee population and identifying parts of the scale that are in need of additional items. Figure 9.5 shows the item map for the exam1 data. The distribution of examinee ability values is shown on the left side of the plot, and the distribution for item difficulty is on the right. For the most part, these two distributions are aligned. Most of the items are located in the region with most examinees. Because of the relationship between item difficulty and the standard error of the ability estimates, most examinees completing this test will be measured with an adequate amount of precision. However, the item map also reveals that there are more extreme persons than there are extreme items. There are examinees with ability values greater than 2.5 but no items with a difficulty larger than 2.2. As a result, high-scoring examinees will be measured with less precision (and more error) than moderate ability examinees. The same trend is evident at the low end of the scale. There are a few examinees with ability values less than −2.0 but no items in this region. The item map in Figure 9.5 makes evident that the test could be improved by adding easier and more difficult items to the test (i.e. $|b| > 2.0$). This change would improve measurement precision at the extreme parts of the scale.

Item maps not only provide an overall summary of items and persons, but also provide a way to develop qualitative description of the latent scale and diagnostic feedback. Huynh and Meyer (2003) provide an example of using an item map for scale description, and Wilson (2005) explains how to use them to develop a rich scale with diagnostic information.

Nonparametric Estimation of Characteristic Curves

As an alternative to estimating model parameters and plotting a curve, you could compute a characteristic curve directly from the data by plotting the proportion of examinees within a small range of sum score levels who endorse the response

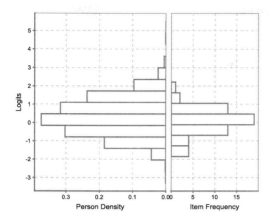

FIGURE 9.5 The item map for exam1 data

option. This function would be jagged and not appear as smooth as the character-istic curves that result from using the Rasch, partial credit, or rating scale model. To overcome this limitation, Ramsay (1991) adapted nonparametric regression for estimating characteristic curves. His approach uses the Nadaraya-Watson estima-tor such that for $i = 1, \ldots, N$ examinees the probability of responding to category k of item j is given by

$$P_{jk}(\theta) = \frac{\sum\limits_{i=1}^{N} K\left(\dfrac{x_i - \theta}{h}\right) y_{ijk}}{\sum\limits_{i=1}^{N} K\left(\dfrac{x_i - \theta}{h}\right)},$$

where K is a kernel function that assigns the most weight to examinees with ability values close to the evaluation point θ and less weight to examinees that are distal from it. The bandwidth, h, influences the distribution of weights and controls the smoothness of the function. Small values for h concentrate the weight in a small region of the scale and can result in a very rough and jagged function. Conversely, large values of the bandwidth spread the weight over a wider region of the scale and result in a smooth function. Choosing a bandwidth is not without consequences. Small bandwidths can produce too much variance, and large band-widths can result in excessive bias. The ideal bandwidth is one that optimizes this bias-variance trade-off, and there are various ways to compute it. Ramsay (2000) recommends using a simple plug-in bandwidth that is proportional to $N^{-1/5}$.

   As will be demonstrated later in the chapter, a benefit of estimating character-istic curves directly from the data is that it can reveal problematic items in ways that a parametric item response model cannot. In addition, it can be applied to all response options of a binary item, not just the correct answer, and it can be used to evaluate differential item functioning (DIF) by computing curves separately for the reference and focal groups.

Running the Analysis in jMetrik

Plotting Item and Test Characteristics

To plot characteristic curves and information functions, you must save the item parameter table from a Rasch analysis. Select the item parameter table in the *Table list* that contains parameters for the items you would like to plot. Click **Graph** → **IrtPlot** from the main menu to start the *Irt Plot dialog* (see Figure 9.6). This dialog includes four panels with options that affect the display of each plot. The *Item panel* includes three checkboxes. Select the *Characteristic curve checkbox* in this panel to plot the item characteristic curve, and choose the *Information function checkbox* to add the item information function to the plot. You can add a legend to the plot by selecting the *Show legend checkbox*.

The *IRT Plot dialog* creates plots for individual items and an overall person plot. The person plot will include the TCC if you select the *Characteristic curve checkbox* in the *Person panel*. The particular TCC it creates depends on the items you select in the dialog. If you select a single item, then the TCC will be the same as the item characteristic curve. If you select all items on the test, then the person plot will contain the TCC for the entire test. These same conventions apply to the TIF. You can plot the TIF or standard error function by selecting the *Information function*

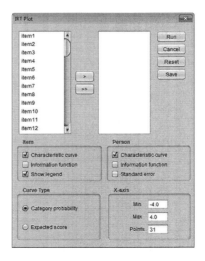

FIGURE 9.6 IRT Plot dialog

checkbox or *Standard error checkbox*, respectively. These two functions will be based on only the items you select for the plots. Note that the values of the standard error function are very different from the values for the characteristic curve and information functions. Therefore, you should include the standard error function in its own plot. Do not select the characteristic curve or information function options when you select the standard error option.

The *Curve Type panel* includes two options that mainly affect the plotting of polytomous items. If you would like to plot category characteristic curves for all options of a polytomous item, then select the *Category probability radio button*. If you would like to see the expected value function instead, then choose the *Expected score radio button*. This latter option is preferred when you aim to include the information function in the plot for a polytomous item. Other than changing the *y*-axis label, this option will not affect the plot for a binary item because the expected value function and the probability of a correct response are the same.

In the *X-axis panel*, you have three options for modifying the *x*-axis of the plots. Type the minimum value in the *Min text field*, and type the maximum in the *Max text field*. By default, jMetrik will use 31 even-spaced points between these minimum and maximum values to compute the probabilities and create the plot. If you would like to use more or fewer evaluation points, then type a different number in the *Point text field*.

After you create a plot in jMetrik, you can save it as an image file (PNG or JPG). Right click the plot and select the *Save As option* from the context menu. Use the dialog that appears to navigate to the folder where you would like to save the file. Type a name for the file in the *File Name text field*, and click the *Save button*. You can repeat these steps for each file you would like to save. However, these steps are tedious if you would like to save a plot for every item on a test. A better alternative is to save all plots as a batch of files. To save all of the plots you create, click the *Save button* in the *IRT Plot dialog*, and select a folder where you would like to save the files. All of the plots will be saved in this location. Each plot will be saved as a JPG file with the same name as the variable name. This method of saving multiple plots will save a substantial amount of work. However, be careful when using this method for saving images. Old files will be automatically overwritten by new files of the same name each time you run the analysis. To avoid overwriting files you would like to keep, choose a different location on your computer each time you elect to save item plots in batch mode.

Creating an Item Map

An item map requires person and item parameter estimates from the Rasch models procedure in jMetrik. To create an item map, select the table that contains the person ability estimates. Next, click **Graph → Item Map** from the main menu to start the *Item Map dialog*. This dialog requires input for the person ability variable and the item parameter table. In the *Variable Selection panel* at the top of the dialog, select the variable that contains the person ability values. Next, click the *Select button* in the *Item Parameter Table panel* to choose the item parameter table. No additional input is required, but if you would like to add a title and subtitle to the plot, click the *Titles button*, and use the dialog that appears to add titles. Finally, click the *Run button* to approve your selections and create the item map.

Creating Nonparametric Curves

Nonparametric curves require that you first create a transformation of the sum score to use as the independent variable in the analysis. Use the test scaling procedures to convert sum scores into van der Waerden normal scores with ties broken randomly (see chapter 3). Select the table with the item responses and this new variable, then click **Graph → Nonparametric curves** to start the *Nonparametric Characteristic Curves dialog* (see Figure 9.7). Three panels in this dialog control the computation and display of the nonparametric curves. The *Kernel Options panel* allows you to choose the type of kernel function in the *Kernel type combo box*. Table 9.1 lists the different kernel functions available in jMetrik. The Gaussian kernel is the default, and it is suitable for most applications. The bandwidth (i.e. smoothing parameter) is computed using $h = 1.1N^{-1/5}Sa$, where N is the total sample size, S is the standard deviation of the independent variable, and a is an adjustment factor. The default value of the adjustment factor is 1, but you can control the amount of smoothing by changing the adjustment factor in the *Bandwidth adjustment text field*. Adjustment values larger than 1 will increase the amount

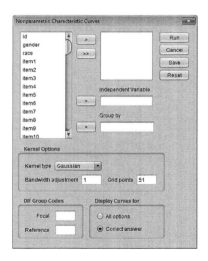

FIGURE 9.7 Nonparametric Characteristic Curves dialog

TABLE 9.1 Kernel functions

Name	Function, $K(u)$
Gaussian	$\dfrac{1}{\sqrt{2\pi}}\exp\left(-\dfrac{1}{2}u^2\right)$
Epanechnikov	$\dfrac{3}{4}(1-u^2)$ for $\lvert u \rvert \leq 1$, 0 otherwise
Uniform	$\dfrac{1}{2}$ for $\lvert u \rvert \leq 1$, 0 otherwise
Triangle	$\left(1-\lvert u \rvert\right)$ for $\lvert u \rvert \leq 1$, 0 otherwise
Biweight	$\dfrac{15}{16}(1-u^2)^2$ for $\lvert u \rvert \leq 1$, 0 otherwise
Triweight	$\dfrac{35}{32}(1-u^2)^3$ for $\lvert u \rvert \leq 1$, 0 otherwise
Cosine	$\dfrac{\pi}{4}\cos\left(\dfrac{\pi}{2}u\right)$ for $\lvert u \rvert \leq 1$, 0 otherwise

of smoothing, and values less than 1 will decrease it. If you make the bandwidth too large, you will get a horizontal line at the average item score (i.e. classical item difficulty level). If you make it too small, you will get a very jagged line that interpolates the average item score at each value of the independent variable. The default bandwidth is adequate for most cases. If anything, you will likely increase it when you have a small sample size. Finally, you can control the number of points at which the function is evaluated by changing the value in the *Grid points text field*. The only reason to change this value is to increase the speed of computation. Smaller numbers will require fewer computations and increase the speed. The default value is ideal for most cases.

You have a choice of computing curves for the expected value or each possible response option. In the *Display Curves for panel*, choose the *Correct answer radio button* (the default) to display the expected value function (i.e. probability of a correct response for a binary item). Alternatively, select the *All options radio button* to create curves for every possible response option. This latter radio button is the preferred way to display curves for polytomous items.

If you wish to conduct a DIF analysis by producing item characteristic curves separately for focal and reference group members, then you need to provide additional input to the *Nonparametric Characteristic Curves dialog*. Select the variable that contains the group membership codes, and move it to the *Group by text field*. Then, type the focal and reference group codes in their respective text fields of the *DIF Group Codes panel*. Complete the remaining parts of the dialog as described previously. When you run the analysis, jMetrik will create two curves for each plot, one for the focal group and one for the reference group. However, jMetrik will not display characteristic curves for all options when you use these steps to conduct a DIF analysis. It defaults to the expected value function for both binary and polytomous items.

Finally, the *Nonparametric Characteristic Curves dialog* allows you to save plots in batch mode using the same steps described previously for IRT plots. Click the *Save button* in the dialog to select a folder where the plots will be saved. Any files in this location with the same name as a new plot will be overwritten.

Example 1: Binary Items

The first example uses the exam1 data to demonstrate the production of characteristic curves for a test composed of binary items. A Rasch model curve and information function for an exam1 item was shown previously in Figure 9.4, and the exam1 data item map was shown earlier in Figure 9.5. For brevity, these figures are not discussed again here. Instead, this example focuses on the nonparametric approach to creating curves to demonstrate the benefits of this type of analysis.

To conduct the analysis, follow the steps outlined above for creating nonparametric curves. Use a van der Waerden normal score for the independent variable, and run the analysis with the default options. Figure 9.8 shows the nonparametric item characteristic curve for item34. It conveys a monotonic nondecreasing relationship between the probability of a correct response and examinee ability. It appears similar to an item characteristic for the Rasch model (e.g. Figure 9.4), but

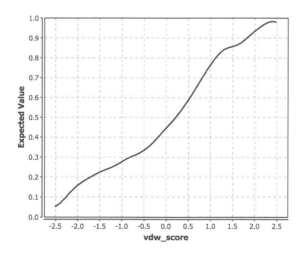

FIGURE 9.8 A nonparametric item characteristic curve

it is not as smooth. It is wavy and has several points of inflection. This waviness does not indicate a problem with the item. Indeed, you can reduce the waviness by increasing the bandwidth. It is simply a product of the nonparametric procedure and a result of imposing very few assumptions on the data.

A benefit of estimating characteristic curves in this manner is that the curve is not required to conform to a parametric model. A characteristic curve for the Rasch model will always be a strictly increasing monotonic function, but the nonparametric curve does not have the same restriction. A nonparametric curve can decrease as examinee ability increases, which indicates a problem with the item. For example, the answer key for item34 was changed to a distractor (i.e. miskeyed) to produce the curve in Figure 9.9. Notice that the characteristic curve decreases as examinees ability increases. It indicates that low-scoring examinees tend to answer the item correctly, but high-scoring examinees do not. This relationship is the opposite of what you should see for an item. It would also be revealed by a negative item discrimination value from a classical item analysis. However, if you applied the Rasch model to this miskeyed item, the resulting characteristic curve would be an increasing function, and you would not see any evidence in the plot that the item was miskeyed. Nonparametric curves are a useful way to identify problematic items because they do not impose a rigid model on the data. They allow the data to speak for themselves.

A second benefit of the nonparametric approach is that it can be applied to the correct response and all of the distractors. This feature allows you to evaluate the overall quality of the item and the performance of each distractor. If there is an order to your distractors, then you will see that each option is the most likely response over a range of ability values. For example, Figure 9.10 shows

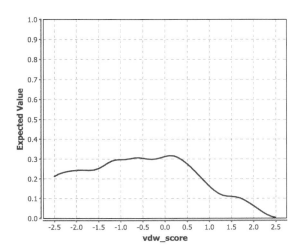

FIGURE 9.9 A nonparametric item characteristic curve for a miskeyed item

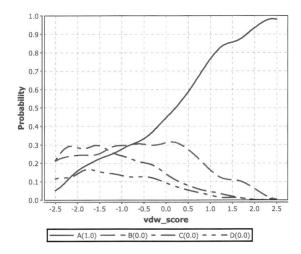

FIGURE 9.10 Nonparametric curves for all response options on a binary item

option characteristic curves for `item34`. Option C is the most likely response for examinees below −1.4, and option B is the most likely response between −1.8 and 1.8. At higher ability levels, the correct answer (option A) is the most probable response. These results show that options B and C are not only plausible distractors, but that there is an order to their degree of plausibility. They stand in contrast with option D. There is no part of the scale where option D is the most likely response. It may be possible to improve this item and reduce the amount of time needed to complete it by eliminating option D.

If there is no apparent order to the distractors over a range of ability levels, the option characteristic curves for them will be similar and show that they are about equally likely. This result will occur when low ability examinees are unable to make use of information in the distractors and simply guess at a response. `Item55` in the exam 1 data (not shown) is an example. All response options for this item are of equal probability until an ability level of about −1.2 where option D becomes the most likely response. It continues to stand out until an ability level of about 0 where the correct answer (option A) becomes the most likely response. Thus, it seems that examinees with very low levels of ability simply guess at the answer, but examinees with moderate levels of ability erroneously cue in to the information in option D. Examinees with high levels of ability are most likely to get the item correct, but option D is the most plausible distractor for them.

Example 2: Mixed Format Test

The second example uses the difsim data to demonstrate the use of nonparametric curves with polytomous items and the illustration of DIF. Figure 9.2 showed option characteristic curves for `item52` in the difsim data. These curves exhibited no sign of a reversal with step parameters that ranged from −1. 2 to 1.2. You can produce similar curves without using the partial credit model or any other item response model. Run the nonparametric curves procedure with the difsim data by first creating a van der Waerden normal score from the sum score with ties broken randomly (see chapter 3). Then, start the *Nonparametric Characteristic Curves dialog*, choose `item52`, and select the newly created normal score as the independent variable. Figure 9.11 shows the curve produced from this analysis. They appear to be quite smooth and similar to the parametric curves for the same item (e.g. Figure 9.2). Although not shown here, the nonparametric curves for `item51`, the other polytomous item on this test, are also similar to the curves based on the partial credit model.

As a final example, nonparametric curves allow you to illustrate the extent of DIF. Recall that in chapter 6, we identified `item5` from the difsim data as an item that had a large amount of DIF in favor of the reference group. To illustrate this result, we can run a DIF analysis with the nonparametric curve procedure. Run the analysis again, but this time select `group` as the *Group by variable*, and enter 1 for the focal group code and 0 for the reference group code. Click the *Run button* to execute the analysis and produce the plot. Figure 9.12 shows that the item is uniformly easier for reference group members than it is for focal group members. The focal group curve is shifted to the right of the reference group curve, which indicates that the item is more difficult for focal group members. Characteristic curves for `item5` stand in contrast to items that do not exhibit DIF. If you plot focal and reference group curves for `item2` (not shown), an item free of DIF,

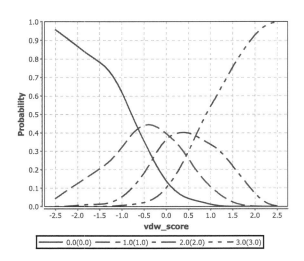

FIGURE 9.11 Nonparametric characteristic curves for a polytomous item

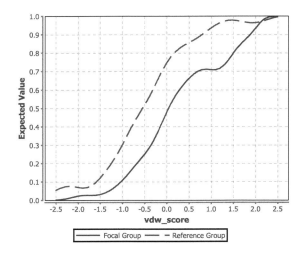

FIGURE 9.12 Nonparametric curve for a DIF analysis

you will see that the curves for each group are much closer and even overlapping in some places.

Nonparametric curves are a good way to illustrate DIF, but they are not a good way to start a DIF analysis. A more useful approach is to evaluate the presence of DIF with the Cochran–Mantel–Haenszel, common odds ratio, and ETS classification levels. Then, use the nonparametric curve procedure to illustrate the extent of DIF for problematic items such as those that are classified as C items.

10

IRT SCALE LINKING AND SCORE EQUATING

Testing programs often use multiple test forms to promote test security and discourage cheating. For this practice to be fair and equitable (Cook & Eignor, 1991), different test forms must measure the same construct, align with the same table of specifications, and have identical statistical characteristics (e.g. difficulty, reliability) for all subgroups of examinees (Lord, 1980). In this way, scores from different test forms are interchangeable, and it would make no difference to an examinee which test form she completed. Unfortunately, this ideal is not easily attainable. Test forms often differ slightly in difficulty even when built to the same specifications. As a result, an examinee that completes the easier test form has an unfair advantage over the student that takes the more difficult test form. Test equating eliminates this unfair advantage by adjusting scores to account for differences in difficulty.

There are classical and modern approaches to test equating (see Kolen & Brennan, 2004). Classical methods focus on equating observed scores, whereas modern approaches involve latent traits and item response theory (IRT). This chapter focuses on IRT methods for scale linking and score equating. In scale linking, IRT parameter estimates are placed on a common scale. This results in comparable examinee proficiency values (i.e. latent trait values). It also results in comparable scale scores as long as the score transformation involves examinee proficiency values. There is no need for equating because linked proficiency values or their scale score transformations are already on a common scale. Equating is only needed in an IRT context when scale scores are a transformation of observed scores. Scale linking is a prerequisite for score equating in IRT. Therefore, this chapter will first discuss linking methods and then describe procedures for score equating. It ends with two examples of running the analysis in jMetrik.

Data Collection Designs

In the simplest case, examinees complete one of two different test forms. Let Form Y be the test form that establishes the scale. It is often referred to as the base test form or old test form. Now let Form X represent a new or alternative test form. The linking will be conducted such that parameter estimates from Form X will be transformed to the scale of Form Y. The linking direction is important. Reversing the direction will produce a different result. jMetrik assumes that Form X is being linked to the scale of Form Y (i.e. an X to Y transformation).

Scale linking requires specific procedures for data collection, and there are two popular methods. In the randomly equivalent groups design, test forms are assigned to each examinee in a random fashion. Examinees taking each test form are considered to be random samples from the same population. Thus, the distribution of scores for the group examinees taking Form X is considered to randomly equivalent to the distribution of scores for the Form Y examinees. The second possible design is referred to as a common item nonequivalent groups design. It is also called the nonequivalent groups with anchor test design. As implied by the name, the groups in this design represent random samples from different populations. They do not have equivalent score distributions. Instead, Form X and Form Y each have a unique set of items and a shared set of items (i.e. the common items or anchor test). The randomly equivalent groups and common item designs are not mutually exclusive. They may be combined by randomly assigning test forms that have common items. Of the two methods, the common item nonequivalent groups design is easier to implement on a large scale and is more popular in practice. For this reason, the remainder of this chapter will focus on the common item design.

Supported Item Response Models

jMetrik provides scale linking and score equating procedures for a wide variety of item response models, but it only estimates parameters for the Rasch family of item response models (e.g. Rasch, partial credit, and rating scale models). To conduct linking and equating with other item response models, you must estimate parameters with a separate program and import the results into jMetrik. The format of the imported item parameter file must follow specific conventions listed in the appendix. With a properly formatted item parameter table, the procedures for scale linking and score equating are the same regardless of whether jMetrik produced the table or you created it with results from another program.

Supported binary item response models include the Rasch model, two-parameter logistic (2PL), and three-parameter logistic (3PL) models. Of these models, the 3PL is the most general. It is given by

$$P(\theta) = c + (1-c)\frac{\exp[Da(\theta - b)]}{1 + \exp[Da(\theta - b)]},$$

where D is a scaling constant that is either 1.0 or 1.7, a is the item discrimina-tion parameter, b is the item difficulty, and c is the lower asymptote (i.e. guessing) parameter. Notice that the 3PL reduces to the Rasch model when $D = 1$, $a = 1$, and $c = 0$, and it reduces to the 2PL when $c = 0$.

Polytomous item response models supported by jMetrik include the rating scale model, partial credit model, generalized partial credit model (GPCM), and graded response model. The GPCM is the most general form of the divide-by-total models (Thissen & Steinberg, 1986). For an item j with $h = 1, \ldots, m_j$ response categories, the probability of the response k is given by

$$P_{jk}(\theta) = \frac{\exp\left[\sum_{v=1}^{k} Da_j(\theta - b_{jv})\right]}{\sum_{h=1}^{m_j}\exp\left[\sum_{v=1}^{h} Da_j(\theta - b_{jv})\right]},$$

where b_{jv} is a step parameter that may be decomposed into an item difficulty parameter and a threshold parameter (see appendix).

Scale Linking

Steps for linking test forms to a common scale differ depending on whether esti-mation is conducted concurrently or separately. In concurrent calibration, data from all test forms are combined into a single data set, and the parameters are esti-mated simultaneously. The overlap in common items will result in estimates that are on a common scale. No further work is needed to place Form X parameter estimates on the scale of Form Y. It is handled automatically during estimation. jMetrik allows you to conduct concurrent calibration with any of the Rasch family of models. After combining the data from each form into a single data file, run the Rasch models analysis described in the chapter on that topic. The estimates for each form will be on a common scale when the analysis completes. Fixed common item calibration is a slight variation that also places parameters on a common scale during the estimation routine. In this procedure, you estimate Form Y parameters and save the results as an item parameter table. Then, you estimate the Form X parameters with the common items fixed to their estimated values on Form Y. Chapter 7 described steps for fixing item parameters to values stored in an item parameter table. Follow those steps to conduct fixed common item calibration.

In separate calibration, parameters for each form are estimated separately, and you must complete additional steps to link estimates to a common scale. Recall that the proficiency scale in IRT is only determined up to a linear transformation. This means that a linear transformation of the item and person parameters will not affect the fit of the model to the data (Kolen & Brennan, 2004). Indeterminacy in the Rasch model is typically resolved by setting the average item difficulty to 0. In other item response models, it is resolved by setting the mean and standard deviation of the person ability distribution to 0 and 1, respectively. A consequence of setting the mean person ability to 0 and standard deviation to 1 during separate estimation of Form X and Form Y parameters is that examinees taking Form X will have the same mean ability level as those taking Form Y even though the two groups may not be equivalent.[1] That is, we end up with within group scales. Form X parameter estimates must be linearly transformed to the scale of Form Y to have a common scale.

For the X to Y transformation, denote Form X parameters with the subscript X and denote Form X parameters transformed to the Form Y scale with the subscript $Y\star$. To adjust the Form X parameters to the scale of Form Y, use the linear transformation $\theta_{Y\star} = A\theta_X + B$ to place a Form X ability, θ_X, on the scale of Form Y. Similar transformations are applied to the item parameters. Discrimination is transformed by $a_{Y\star} = a_X/A$, and difficulty and step parameters are transformed by $b_{Y\star} = Ab_X + B$. In each of these transformations, the scale and intercept coefficients are denoted as A and B. Note that the opposite transformation (i.e. the Y to X transformation) is often needed to implement the characteristic curve methods. In these cases, Form Y difficulty is transformed to the Form X scale using $b_{X\#} = (b_Y - B)/A$, and the Form Y discrimination is transformed to the Form X scale using $a_{X\#} = Aa_Y$.

Separate calibration linking procedures involve four different methods for obtaining these transformation coefficients. They are the mean/sigma, mean/mean, Stocking-Lord, and Haebara methods. The mean/sigma (Loyd & Hoover, 1980) and mean/mean (Marco, 1977) methods are referred to as method of moments procedures because they use only item parameter descriptive statistics to compute the transformation coefficients. They are easy to implement and can be computed by hand. For example, mean/sigma transformation coefficients can be computed from the summary statistics. The slope coefficient is computed from the common item estimates by dividing the standard deviation of Form Y item difficulty by the standard deviation of Form X item difficulty, $A = \sigma(b_Y)/\sigma(b_X)$. The intercept coefficient is the mean item difficulty of Form Y subtracted by the rescaled Form X mean item difficulty, $B = \mu(b_Y) - A\mu(b_X)$. The mean/sigma method gets its name because it uses the mean and standard deviation of item difficulty parameters. The mean/mean method, on the other hand, only uses the item discrimination and item difficulty means. It does not involve the computation of standard deviations. Specifically, the slope coefficient for the mean/mean method is $A = \mu(a_X)/\mu(a_Y)$. The intercept is computed in the same way as in the mean/sigma method.

Method of moments procedures are attractive because of their simplicity, but they do not make complete use of item characteristics, and they are affected by outliers. Characteristic curve methods overcome these limitations, but they are computer intensive and require specialized software such as jMetrik. The Haebara (Haebara, 1980) and Stocking-Lord (Stocking & Lord, 1983) characteristic curve methods find the transformation coefficients that minimize an objective function. The Haebara method (HB) aims to find transformation coefficients (A and B) that minimize a function of the sum of the squared differences in item characteristic curves:

$$ HB = \sum_{i=1}^{n} \left\{ \sum_{j=1}^{p} \left[P_{Yj}(\theta_i) - P_{Yj}^{\star}(\theta_i; A, B) \right]^2 \right\} f(\theta_i) $$
$$ + \sum_{i=1}^{n} \left\{ \sum_{j=1}^{p} \left[P_{Xj}(\theta_i) - P_{Xj}^{\#}(\theta_i; A, B) \right]^2 \right\} q(\theta_i). $$

In this criterion function, $P_Y^{\star}(\theta_i; A, B)$ is a Form X item characteristic curve with parameters transformed to the scale of Form Y. It represents the X to Y transformation. Similarly, $P_X^{\#}(\theta_i; A, B)$ is a Form Y item characteristic curve with parameters transformed to the scale of Form X. It represents the Y to X transformation. In minimizing HB with respect to A and B, the Haebara method finds the transformation that makes the Form X common item characteristic curves as similar as possible to the Form Y common item curves.

The Stocking-Lord (SL) procedure is similar to the Haebara method, but it aims to find the transformation coefficients (A and B) that minimize a function of the sum of squared differences in test characteristic curves:

$$ SL = \sum_{i=1}^{n} \left[T_Y(\theta_i) - T_Y^{\star}(\theta_i; A, B) \right]^2 f(\theta_i) $$
$$ + \sum_{i=1}^{n} \left[T_X(\theta_i) - T_X^{\#}(\theta_i; A, B) \right]^2 q(\theta_i). $$

In this function, $T_Y(\theta)$ indicates the Form Y common item test characteristic curve (i.e. the sum of Form Y common item expected values) and $T_Y^{\star}(\theta; A, B)$ is the Form X common item test characteristic curve with parameters transformed to the scale of Form Y. It represents the X to Y transformation. The second term on the right side of SL includes the Form X common item test characteristic curve, $T_X(\theta)$, and the Form Y test characteristic curve with parameter transformed to the scale of Form X, $T_X^{\#}(\theta; A, B)$. This part represents the Y to X transformation. Although the original Stocking-Lord procedure only involved the X to Y transformation terms, Kim and Kolen (2007) added the Y to X terms to produce a symmetric linking function. In minimizing SL with respect to A and B, the Stocking-Lord procedure finds the transformation that makes the Form X common item test characteristic curve as similar as possible to the Form Y common item test characteristic curve.

In HB and SL, the summation is done over a distribution of $i = 1, \ldots, n$ proficiency values. The sum of squared differences in X to Y transformation terms is taken over the distribution of Form Y examinees as indicated by the Form Y distribution function $f(\theta)$. Likewise, the sum of squared differences in Y to X transformation terms is taken over the distribution of Form X examinees, $q(\theta)$. jMetrik gives you three options related to the summation in SL and HB. First, symmetric minimization minimizes HB and SL as shown previously. The second option is backward (X to Y) minimization. It only uses the first term on the right side of HB or SL. Finally, forward minimization (Y to X) uses only the second term on the right-hand side of HB or SL. Symmetric minimization is the default option.

Among the various methods for scale linking, the Stocking-Lord procedure works best when items are all of the same type (Baker & Al-Karni, 1991; Wells, Subkoviak, & Serlin, 2002), and the Haebara method works best in mixed format tests with binary and polytomous items (Kim & Lee, 2006). Concurrent calibration and fixed common item procedures also work very well (Hanson & Béguin, 2002), particularly when compared to the method of moments procedures. However, these two methods make it difficult to detect items that have an undue influence on linking process.

Checking Parameter Invariance

As discussed in chapter 7, item parameters are invariant up to a linear transformation. The distribution of examinees does not affect the item characteristic curve. However, invariance is a property of the model parameters, not the parameter estimates. Therefore, you must test for a lack of invariance (LOI) in common item parameter estimates prior to scale linking. jMetrik provides the robust z procedure for testing LOI. This method allows the discrimination and difficulty (or step) parameters to be evaluated independently. It first tests for LOI in item discrimination parameters and then tests for LOI in item difficulty or step parameters. Let d_j be the difference in item parameters (either discrimination or difficulty) for common item j, M be the median of the differences, and IQR be the interquartile range of the differences. Robust z is then $z_j = [d_j - M]/0.74IQR$. This statistic is asymptotically distributed as a standard normal deviate. If the absolute value of z_j is 1.645 or larger, the item is flagged as exhibiting LOI (e.g. it is a drifting or outlying item). Simulation studies show that robust z test has an inflated type I error rate (Green, Smith, & Habing, 2010; Meyer & Huynh, 2010). Therefore, a larger cutoff value such as 1.96 or 2.7 is also acceptable (Huynh & Meyer, 2010).

When using robust z with item response models that have a discrimination parameter, the test proceeds in two steps. First, the discrimination parameters are tested using the difference $d_j = \log(a_{Yj}) - \log(a_{Xj})$. A scale transformation coefficient (i.e. A) is computed by taking the exponent of the mean difference for items that have a robust z value less than the cutoff value, $A = \exp(\bar{d})$. Next, the item difficulty parameters are tested using the difference $d_j = b_{Yj} - Ab_{Xj}$. Any item that shows a LOI at either step is one that should be removed from the pool of common items. Robust z should not be used iteratively each time an item is removed from the pool. It should only be applied to the initial pool of common items.

In addition to using robust z to evaluate individual items for LOI, you should also consider the quality of the entire set of common items. Huynh (2009) explains that parameter estimates for the common items should be highly related and show a similar level of variation on each test form. Specifically, he indicated that Form X difficulty estimates should correlate 0.95 or higher with Form Y difficulty estimates, and the standard deviation ratio for item difficulty, $\hat{\sigma}(b_Y) / \hat{\sigma}(b_X)$, should be between 0.9 and 1.1. Item discrimination estimates among common items on each form should also be highly related and show similar variation. However, a slightly lower correlation and a wider range of standard deviation ratios are acceptable. Taherbhai and Seo (2013) note that no more than 20% of the common items should be eliminated from the pool. They recommend eliminating the common items with the largest robust z values first and only eliminating items if the correlation between common item parameter estimates is less than 0.95 and the standard deviation ratio is outside the acceptable range.

True Score Equating

In some testing programs, scale scores are a transformation of the sum score and not IRT proficiency estimates. Therefore, the sum scores must be adjusted for differences in test form difficulty through equating. IRT true score equating is a method that allows you to equate sum scores on Form X to the sum scores on Form Y (Kolen & Brennan, 2004). It involves the test characteristic curve for each test form. The test characteristic curve is the sum of the item characteristic curves, and it describes the regression of true scores on the latent trait. Let $\tau_Y(\theta)$ denote the test characteristic curve for Form Y, and $\tau_X(\theta)$ denote the test characteristic curve for Form X. This notation differs from the notion in the equation for SL to indicate the test characteristic curve for the entire test form, not just the common items. The Form Y equivalent of a Form X true score is given by $\tau_Y^*(\theta) = \tau_Y(\tau_X^{-1})$, where τ_X^{-1} is the IRT proficiency value that corresponds to the Form X true score. Although this equating is easy to illustrate by plotting the two test characteristic curves on the same chart, it actually requires numerical procedures to implement it in practice. jMetrik uses the Newton-Raphson procedure to find τ_X^{-1} (see Kolen & Brennan, 2004). This procedure is repeated for all possible true score values. As a result of true score equating, Form Y equivalents and the Form Y true scores are now on the same scale and have been adjusted for difficulty. They may be transformed to scale scores for reporting.

Running the Analysis in jMetrik

Unlike other methods in jMetrik, you do not need to select a data table before starting the dialog. Click **Transform → IRT Scale Linking** to start the *Scale Linking dialog* (see Figure 10.1). The *Parameters tab* includes four panels, but the only required input is information in the *Item Parameters panel*. Click the *Select Form X button* in the *Item Parameters panel* to display a list of available tables. Choose the Form X item parameter table, and click the *OK button*. Now click the *Select Form Y button* to display a list of available tables. Choose the Form Y item parameter table from the list, and click the *OK button*. Thus far, you have provided the Form X and Y table names, but you have not provided information about the common items. Common items can have different names on each test form. The *X-Y Pairs dialog* allows you to match the common items on each form. Click the *Select XY Pairs button* to display the *X-Y Pairs dialog*. You will see two lists of item names. Select a Form X name and a Form Y name to identify the same common item on each form. Click the *Select button* to move the item pair to the *X-Y Item Pairs list*. Repeat these steps for each common item. Press the *OK button* to accept your input and return to the *IRT Scale Linking dialog*. You can run the

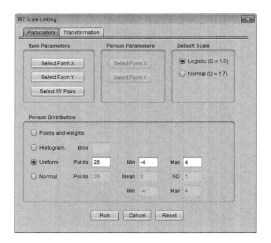

FIGURE 10.1 Parameters tab in the Scale Linking dialog

analysis with no additional input by clicking the *Run button.* jMetrik will compute summary statistics and the transformation coefficients, but it will not make any transformation at this point.

Recall that characteristic curve methods involve a sum over the Form Y and Form X distribution. The *Person Distribution panel* is where you provide information about these distributions. The default person distribution in jMetrik uses 25 evenly spaced points from a uniform distribution that ranges from −4 to 4. You can change this default to a normal distribution or values stored in a table. Select the *Normal radio button* to use 25 evenly spaced points from a normal distribution with a mean of 0 and a standard deviation of 1. You can change the number of points, range of values, mean, and standard deviation for the normal distribution by changing the values in the text fields.

jMetrik gives you two options for supplying your own person distribution values that are stored in a table. The first option is designed for input in the form of quadrature points and weights. It allows you to provide information about the posterior distribution of ability that is often output by IRT programs. To provide input about existing points (required) and weights (required), choose the *Points and weights radio button.* This action will activate buttons in the *Person Parameters panel.* Press the *Select Form X button* in the *Person Parameters panel* to display the *Form X Person Parameters dialog.* You will see a list of table names on the left side of this dialog. Click the table that contains the variable with person ability points. Select the variable from the list of variable names (i.e. the list in the middle of the dialog), and press the *Select button* to move it to the *Theta text field.* If you do not have weights, you can press the *OK button* to accept your selection. Otherwise, select the variable that contains the weights, and then press the second *Select button* to move the variable to the *Weight text field.* Click *OK* to accept your selections. Repeat these steps for the Form Y ability values.

The second option for providing information about examinees is the histogram option. This option allows you to provide individual examinee ability values instead of quadrature points and weights. jMetrik will summarize this information into a histogram before executing the scale linking analysis. To use this option, choose the *Histogram radio button,* and type a number (e.g. 10) in the text field that appears next to the radio button. The histogram option will summarize observed proficiency values into a histogram with the number of bins that you specify. It will then use the bin midpoints and density values from this histogram as the quadrature points and weights, respectively, when conducting the characteristic curve methods. After providing person distribution information, click the *Run button* to execute the analysis.

The final option on the *Parameters tab* of the *IRT Scale Linking* dialog is straightforward. It applies to the default value of the scaling constant D in item response models. The default is $D = 1.0$ for the logistic metric, but you can also choose $D = 1.7$ for the normal metric. Your choice should match the scaling constant used during parameter estimation. The selected value is a default that will be overwritten by the value of the scale variable in an item parameter table. That is, the selected option in the *Default Scale panel* only applies to item parameter tables that omit the scale variable or items in the item parameter table that do not have an entry for the scale variable.

The *Transformation tab* includes five panels that allow you to configure options and specify the method for transforming item and person parameters (see Figure 10.2). jMetrik will compute transformation coefficients for all four methods, but it will only use one method to transform parameters. The *Method panel* provides four options for the transformation method: mean/sigma, mean/mean, Haebara, and Stocking-Lord (the default). Choose the transformation method in this panel, but keep in mind that nothing will actually be transformed until you make a selection in the *Transform panel*.

If you would like to transform Form X item parameters, choose the *Item parameters checkbox* in the *Transform panel*. This option will produce a new item parameter table by copying the original Form X item parameter table and replacing the original item parameter values with their transformed values. The new table will have the same name as the original item parameter table with the addition of the text "_T" to denote a transformed data table.

You have two options for transforming person parameters. The first option is via the *Transform panel*, and the second option is to use the linear transformation analysis described in chapter 3. To use the first option, click the *Person parameters checkbox* to transform person parameters. This option will add a new variable to the Form X data table that you selected in the *Person Parameter panel* on the *Parameters tab* of the dialog. The new variable will have the same name as the original

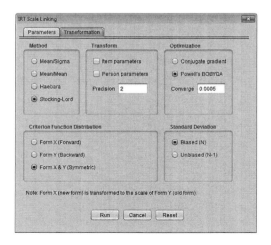

FIGURE 10.2 Transformation tab in the Scale Linking dialog

Form X person ability variable plus the addition of the text "_T" to indicate a transformed value. Person parameter transformation only works if you have selected the *Points and weights radio button* or *Histogram radio button* on the *Parameters tab*. It will have no effect if you have selected the *Uniform* or *Normal radio button*.

The second option for transforming person parameters is more flexible. Select the table that contains the person parameters that you wish to transform, then click **Transform → Linear Transformation** in the main menu. Select the variable that contains the person parameters, and type a new name for the variable that will contain the transformed values. To make the transformation, select a set of transformation coefficients from the IRT Scale Linking output (e.g. the *A* and *B* value for Stocking-Lord), and enter them as the mean and standard deviation in the *Linear Transformation panel*. Enter the *B* coefficient as the mean and the *A* coefficient as the standard deviation. Click the *Run button* to make the transformation, and add the variable of transformed values to the table.

The remaining three panels on the *Transformation tab* provide options for computational aspects of the transformation. In the *Optimization panel*, you can select either the conjugate gradient or Powell's BOBYQA method for minimizing the characteristic curve criterion functions. Although these two methods should produce the same results, the latter method (the default) has performed better in testing. The *Criterion Function Distribution panel* gives you options for forward, backward, or symmetric (the default) summation in computation of the criterion function. Technical aspects of these options were described previously in the chapter. Finally, the *Standard Deviation panel* relates to the method of computing the standard deviation in the mean/sigma procedure and the summary statistics. You can either use a biased estimate with N in the denominator of the standard deviation or an unbiased estimate with $N - 1$ in the denominator. These two options will produce very similar results with a large number of common items.

True Score Equating

To start the *IRT Score Equating dialog* (see Figure 10.3), click **Transform → IRT Score Equating** in the main menu. You do not need to select a table before starting the dialog. You will select the needed tables from within the dialog itself. In the *Item Parameters panel*, click the *Select Form X button* to display a dialog that allows you to select the Form X item parameter table. In the selection dialog that appears, click the name of the Form X item parameter table in the list on the left side of the dialog. This table should contain the Form X parameters that are on the Form Y scale, not the original Form X parameters. That is, it should use the item parameter table that is created during the scale linking analysis. The list in the middle of the dialog will display the item names from selected item parameter table. Choose all items that will be included in computation of the Form X test characteristic curve. You should select all Form X items in this list, not just the common items.

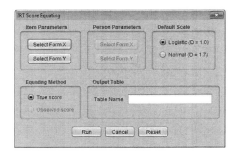

FIGURE 10.3 IRT Score Equating dialog

Once you have selected all Form X items, press the *OK button* to accept your selections. Repeat this process for the Form Y items. As with Form X, your Form Y item selections should include all Form Y items, not just the common items.

jMetrik will create a table that lists Form X scores and their Form Y equivalent scores when you run this analysis. It will display this table in plain text and create a new database table that contains the score conversions. To name the output table, type a name in the *Table Name text field* of the *Output Table panel*. A table with that name will be added to the database when the analysis is finished. There is no other required input for score equating. Press the *Run button* to execute the analysis.

The remaining panels in the *IRT Score Equating dialog* are either optional or inactive. The *Default Scale panel* allows you to select the default scale. These options function in the same way as the *Default Scale panel* options in the *IRT Scale Linking dialog*. There are two inactive buttons in the *Person Parameters panel* and one inactive button in the *Equating Method panel*. These buttons will be active when IRT observed score equating is added to jMetrik. Ignore these buttons for now.

Example 1: Linking with 3PL Items

Example 1 uses the equating4 data sets. These data are 3PL item parameters for two forms of a 30-item test. Item and person parameter estimates were obtained from the program IRT Command Language (ICL; Hanson, 2002). The 8 common items are named `item1`, `item5`, `item9`, `item13`, `item17`, `item21`, `item25`, and `item29` on both forms. You must import three different files for this example. Two files are item parameter files, and one contains the person quadrature points and weights. Import the file of Form X item parameters ("formx-items.txt"), and name it EQ4_X_ITEMS. Import the file of Form Y item parameters ("formy-items.txt"), and name the table EQ4_Y_ITEMS. Finally, import the file of person quadrature points and weights ("xy-person-distribution.txt"), and name it EQ4_PERSON_DIST. You will use all three tables in this example.

The initial analysis will involve all common items and focus on the quality of the common items. Run the IRT scale linking analysis with the points and weights option that allows you to use the quadrature points and weights in the EQ4_PERSON_DIST table. Figure 10.4 shows the portion of output that describes the quality of the common items. The correlation among common item difficulty estimates is 0.99, and the standard deviation ratio is inside the range of acceptable values at 0.98. For the discrimination parameters, the correlation is high (0.93), and the standard deviation ratio is slightly outside the acceptable range at 1.34. Robust z statistics shown in Figure 10.4 provide more insight into the performance of common items. Item21 has a large robust z value for item difficulty (2.46) and item discrimination (−2.59). This item is a candidate for removal from the common item pool. Indeed, this is the only item we can remove and meet our requirement for not removing more than 20% of the common item pool.

Run the analysis again but without item21. To remove this item from the common item pool, start the *IRT Scale Linking dialog*, and click the *Select XY Pairs button*. The list of items you selected earlier will be visible in the *X-Y Item Pairs list* on the right side of this dialog. Click the item21_item21 pair, and press the *Unselect button* to remove this pair from the pool of common items. Click the *OK button* to accept your changes and return to the *IRT Scale Linking dialog*. Press the *Run button* to execute the analysis. Summary statistics for the common items show an improvement with the elimination of item21. The item difficulty correlation is even closer to 1, and the standard deviation ratio is still acceptable at 0.97. There was a slight decrease in the item discrimination correlation, but it rounds to the same value as before (0.93). The standard deviation ratio

```
            Correlation and SD Ratio
========================================
  Parameter            r          Sy/Sx
----------------------------------------
Difficulty          0.9926       0.9763
Discrimination      0.9347       1.3372
========================================


        Robust z Test for Item Discrimination
==================================================
Item Pair                    z       pvalue    Sig
--------------------------------------------------
item1_item1              -0.1135     0.4548
item5_item5               0.1135     0.4548
item9_item9              -1.1192     0.1315
item13_item13            -0.3783     0.3526
item17_item17             0.4354     0.3316
item21_item21             2.4623     0.0069     *
item25_item25            -1.3584     0.0880
item29_item29             0.3633     0.3582
==================================================


      Robust z Test for Item (step) Difficulty
==================================================
Item Pair                    z       pvalue    Sig
--------------------------------------------------
item1_item1              -0.4393     0.3302
item5_item5              -0.1450     0.4424
item9_item9               0.6090     0.2713
item13_item13             0.7339     0.2315
item17_item17             0.1450     0.4424
item21_item21            -2.5914     0.0048     *
item25_item25             0.1761     0.4301
item29_item29            -0.9877     0.1617
==================================================
```

FIGURE 10.4 Common item summary tables for equating4 data

```
                    TRANSFORMATION COEFFICIENTS
              Form X (New Form) to Form Y (Old Form)
================================================================
Method              Slope (A)        Intercept (B)
----------------------------------------------------------------
Mean/Mean             0.98              0.50
Mean/Sigma            0.97              0.49
Haebara               0.93              0.57
Stocking-Lord         0.93              0.57
================================================================
```

FIGURE 10.5 Transformation coefficients

is now 1.14 and within the acceptable range. The robust z statistics should not be computed iteratively. Therefore, we ignore the robust z statistic in this second run. Figure 10.5 lists the transformation coefficients computed from the six common items (i.e. without `item21`).

`Item21` appears to have an adverse effect on the quality of the common item pool. Common item correlations and standard deviation ratios are better without it. Therefore, keep it out of the common item pool, and run the analysis for a third time to transform the Form X parameters using the Stocking-Lord method. Start the *IRT Scale Linking dialog*, and click the *Transformation tab*. Select the *Item parameters checkbox* in the *Transform panel*, and click the *Run button*. The output will be exactly the same as it was from the second run, but now a new table appears in the list named EQ4_X_ITEMS_T. This table contains the Form X parameters transformed to the scale of Form Y.

Example 2: Linking and Equating with 3PL and GPCM Items

Example 2 uses the equating-mixed data to conduct IRT scale linking and true score equating. These data are from a mixed format test that includes 30 binary items and 5 four-category polytomous items on each form. The 9 common items are named `item1`, `item5`, `item9`, `item13`, `item17`, `item21`, `item25`, `item29`, and `item31` on both forms. Responses from 15,000 examinees were calibrated using a 3PL model for the binary items and a GPCM model for the polytomous items. Estimates for both forms were obtained from the software PARSCALE (Muraki & Bock, 2003). You must import the two item parameter files in the eqmixed data sets for this example. Import the Form X file "eqmixed-formX-ipar.csv," and name it EQMIXED_X_ITEMS. Import the Form Y file "eqmixed-formY-ipar.csv," and name it EQMIXED_Y_ITEMS. There are no person parameter files or quadrature points and weights files. Use the default uniform distribution option for the analysis.

Figure 10.6 lists the robust z results and transformation coefficients from the analysis. Item5 has a large robust z value for item difficulty, and `item25` and `item29` have a large robust z value for item discrimination. These items are candidates for removal. However, the common item correlations and standard deviation ratios are all acceptable. Item difficulty has a correlation of 1.0, and item discrimination has a correlation of 0.92. The standard deviation ratio is 1.02 and

```
              Robust z Test for Item Discrimination
======================================================================
Item Pair                              z           pvalue      Sig
----------------------------------------------------------------------
item1_item1                        -1.0110          0.1560
item5_item5                        -2.8564          0.0021        *
item9_item9                        -0.4366          0.3312
item13_item13                       0.1477          0.4413
item17_item17                       0.0000          0.5000
item21_item21                      -0.7221          0.2351
item25_item25                       0.7713          0.2203
item29_item29                       0.9606          0.1684
item31_item31                       0.1983          0.4214
======================================================================


              Robust z Test for Item (step) Difficulty
======================================================================
Item Pair                              z           pvalue      Sig
----------------------------------------------------------------------
item1_item1                         0.5671          0.2853
item5_item5                         1.6209          0.0525
item9_item9                        -0.1660          0.4341
item13_item13                      -0.1612          0.4360
item17_item17                      -0.0934          0.4628
item21_item21                       0.7055          0.2403
item25_item25                      -3.9195          0.0000        *
item29_item29                      -4.3753          0.0000        *
item31_item31_1                     1.1853          0.1179
item31_item31_2                     1.7879          0.0369
item31_item31_3                     0.0000          0.5000
======================================================================


                   TRANSFORMATION COEFFICIENTS
              Form X (New Form) to Form Y (Old Form)
======================================================================
Method             Slope (A)          Intercept (B)
----------------------------------------------------------------------
Mean/Mean            1.00                 0.35
Mean/Sigma           1.02                 0.36
Haebara              0.99                 0.37
Stocking-Lord        1.00                 0.38
======================================================================
```

FIGURE 10.6 Scale linking output for a mixed format test

1.11 for difficulty and discrimination, respectively. These statistics provide evidence that all common items should be retained in the analysis.

To determine whether the common item pool can be improved, remove item29, the common item with the worst robust z statistic for item difficulty, and run the analysis again. The common item correlation and standard deviation ratio for item difficulty looks fine with both values within the acceptable range. However, the item discrimination correlation drops to 0.89, which is too low. This result provides further evidence that we should keep all of the common items and use the transformation coefficients in Figure 10.6. Run the analysis again with all of the original common items. Select the *Item parameters checkbox* on the *Transformation tab* to create a new table with the Form X transformed item parameter values. jMetrik will create the table EQMIXED_X_ITEMS_T with the transformed item parameter values.

To conduct true score equating, start the *IRT Score Equating dialog*. Press the *Select Form X button* to start the item selection dialog. Select the table EQMIXED_X_ITEMS_T in the list on the left of this dialog, and then choose all of the Form X items, not just the common items. Click the *OK button* to accept your selections. Press the *Select Form Y button*, and choose all of the items in the table EQMIXED_Y_ITEMS. Type a name for the output table, and press the *Run button* to execute the analysis.

Figure 10.7 show a portion of the output table. The columns in this table are as follows: (a) "Score" is the original Form X true score, (b) "Theta" is the Form

		SCORE TABLE		
Score	Theta	Y-Equiv	Round	Conv
0	-99.0000	0.0000	0	-
1	-99.0000	0.9803	1	-
2	-99.0000	1.9605	2	-
3	-99.0000	2.9408	3	-
4	-99.0000	3.9210	4	-
5	-99.0000	4.9013	5	-
6	-99.0000	5.8815	6	-
7	-4.0377	6.7315	7	Y
8	-3.2427	7.6079	8	Y
9	-2.7958	8.4802	8	Y
10	-2.4787	9.3541	9	Y
11	-2.2272	10.2384	10	Y
12	-2.0142	11.1390	11	Y
13	-1.8257	12.0577	12	Y
14	-1.6543	12.9931	13	Y
...	...	...	...	...
37	1.2750	36.4236	36	Y
38	1.4526	37.5804	38	Y
39	1.6522	38.7390	39	Y
40	1.8824	39.8917	40	Y
41	2.1573	41.0288	41	Y
42	2.5038	42.1375	42	Y
43	2.9826	43.2008	43	Y
44	3.7906	44.1901	44	Y
45	99.0000	45.0000	45	-

FIGURE 10.7 Score equating output for a mixed format test

X theta value at the true score value, (c) "Y-Equiv" is the Form Y true score equivalent of the Form X true score, (d) "Round" is the Y-Equiv value rounded to the nearest integer, and (e) "Conv" indicates whether the Newton-Raphson procedure converged (Y) or not (N) or is not applicable (–). Notice that some Theta values are listed as −99 and 99. The value −99 is assigned to any Form X true score that is less than the lowest possible true score (i.e. the sum of item guessing parameters). Form Y equivalents for these values are obtained through linear interpolation (Kolen & Brennan, 2004). At the upper end of the scale, the theta value 99 is assigned to the highest possible true score on Form X because it is impossible to estimate examinee proficiency for a perfect score. Therefore, the highest possible true score on Form X is equivalent to the highest possible true score on Form Y.

Figure 10.7 shows that Form X was more difficult than Form Y. For example, a true score of 13 on Form X is equivalent to a true score of 12 on Form Y. Indeed, a review of all scores from the analysis shows that Form X true scores are almost always 1 point larger than their Form Y equivalent scores. Output from the IRT score equating analysis is saved in a database table with the name you provided. You can use this output table to convert Form Y equivalent scores to scale scores using the linear transformation analysis. In the end, you will have a table that shows the raw to scale score conversion.

Note

1 A similar line of reasoning applies when fixing the mean item difficulty to zero.

APPENDIX: ITEM PARAMETER TABLE FORMAT REQUIREMENTS

This table describes the column names and column values in an item parameter table.

Name	Description of Column Values
name	(required) A unique item name
model	(required) A code to indicate the type of item response theory model. Options include the following: L3—One-, two-, and three-parameter binary item response models. PC1—Partial credit and generalized partial credit model as used in ICL software, where the step parameter is $b_{jv} = b_{jv}$. PC2—Partial credit and generalized partial credit model as used in Parscale software. The step parameter is $b_{jv} = b_j + \tau_v$. PC3—Partial credit model or rating scale model as used in Winsteps and jMetrik software, where the step parameter is $b_{jv} = b_j - \tau_v$. GR—Graded response model as in Multilog software. The step parameter is $b_{jv} = b_{jv}$, and it indicates the location of the curve for responding in category v or higher.
ncat	(required) Number of response categories. For binary items, ncat = 2. A three-category polytomous item is ncat = 3, a four-category polytomous item is ncat = 4, etc.
sweight	A space-delimited list of score weights for polytomous items. jMetrik will use default score weights that start at 0 and end with $m - 1$, where m is the number of categories (i.e. ncat = m).
scale	Scaling factor. If omitted, scale = 1.0. For normal metric, use scale = 1.7. For logistic metric, use scale = 1.0.
aparam	Item discrimination parameter. If omitted, aparam = 1.

(Continued)

Name	*Description of Column Values*
bparam	Item difficulty parameter. (Required if model = L3, PC2, or PC3.)
cparam	Lower asymptote (i.e. pseudo-guessing). If omitted, cparam = 0.
stepk	Step or threshold parameter for $k = 1,..., m - 1$ categories. For example, the names for a four-category item would be: *step1*, *step2*, *step3*. The step parameter for the first category (*step0*) is assumed to be 0 and omitted. (Required if ncat > 2.)

REFERENCES

Allen, M. J., & Yen, W. M. (1979). *Introduction to measurement theory*. Belmont, CA: Wadsworth.

American Educational Research Association, American Psychological Association, & National Council on Measurement in Education. (1999). *Standards for educational and psychological testing*. Washington, DC: American Educational Research Association.

Andrich, D. (1978). Rating formulation for ordered response categories. *Psychometrika, 43*(4), 561–573.

Ankenmann, R. D., Witt, E. A., & Dunbar, S. B. (1999). An investigation of the power of the likelihood ratio goodness-of-fit statistic in detecting differential item funcitoning. *Journal of Educational Measurement, 36*, 277–300.

Baker, F. B., & Al-Karni, A. (1991). A comparison of two procedures for computing IRT equating coefficients. *Journal of Educational Measurement, 28*, 147–162.

Bond, T. G., & Fox, C. M. (2007). *Applying the Rasch model: Fundamental measurement in the human sciences* (2nd ed.). Mahwah, NJ: Lawrence Erlbaum.

Brennan, R. L., & Wan, L. (2004). A bootstrap procedure for estimating decision consistency for single-administration complex assessments. Iowa City, IA: Center for Advanced Studies in Measurement and Assessment.

Brown, W. (1910). Some experimental results in the correlation of mental abilities. *British Journal of Psychology, 3*, 296–322.

Cizek, G. J., & Bunch, M. B. (2007). *Standard setting: A guide to establishing and evaluating performance standards for tests*. Thousand Oaks, CA: Sage.

Clauser, B. E., & Mazor, K. M. (1998). Using statistical procedures to identify differentially functioning test items. *Educational Measurement: Issues and Practice, 17*, 31–44.

Cochran, W. G. (1954). Some methods for strengthening the common χ^2 tests. *Biometrics, 10*, 417–451.

Cohen, J. (1960). A coefficient for agreement for nominal scales. *Educational and Psychological Measurement, 20*(1), 37–46.

Cook, L. L., & Eignor, D. R. (1991). An NCME module on IRT equating methods. *Educational Measurement: Issues and Practice, 10*(3), 191–199.

Crocker, L., & Algina, J. (1986). *Introduction to classical and modern test theory.* New York, NY: Holt, Rinehart and Winston.

Cronbach, L. J., & Shavelson, R. J. (2004). My current thoughts on coefficient alpha and successor procedures. *Educational and Psychological Measurement, 64,* 391–418.

Cronbach, L. J., & Warrington, W. G. (1952). Efficiency of multiple-choice tests as a function of spread of item difficulties. *Psychometrika, 17,* 127–147. doi: 10.1007/BF02288778

de Ayala, R. J. (2009). *The theory and practice of item response theory.* New York, NY: Guilford Press.

Donoghue, J. R., & Allen, N. L. (1993). Thin versus thick matching in the Mantel-Haenszel procedure for detecting DIF. *Journal of Educational Statistics, 18,* 131–154.

Dorans, N. J., & Schmitt, A. P. (1991). *Constructed response and differential item functioning: A pragmatic approach* (ETS Research Report 91-47). Princeton, NJ: Educational Testing Service.

Dorans, N. J., Schmitt, A. P., & Belistein, C. A. (1992). The standardization approach to assessing comprehensive differential item functioning. *Journal of Educational Measurement, 29,* 309–319.

Embretson, S. E., & Reise, S. P. (2000). *Item response theory for psychologists.* Mahwah, NJ: Lawrence Erlbaum.

Feldt, L. S. (1975). Estimation of the reliability of a test divided into two parts of unequal length. *Psychometrika, 40,* 557–561.

Feldt, L. S. (2002). Estimating the internal consistency reliability of tests composed of testlets varying in length. *Applied Measurement in Education, 15*(1), 33–48.

Feldt, L. S., & Brennan, R. L. (1989). Reliability. In R. L. Linn (Ed.), *Educational measurement* (3rd ed., pp. 105–146). New York, NY: American Council on Education and MacMillan.

Feldt, L. S., Woodruff, D. J., & Salih, F. A. (1987). Statistical inference for coefficient alpha. *Applied Psychological Measurement, 11,* 93–103.

Gilmer, J. S., & Feldt, L. S. (1983). Reliability estimation for a test with parts of unknown length. *Psychometrika, 48,* 99–111.

Green, J., Smith, J., & Habing, B. (2010). *A comparison of the robust z, Mantel-Haenszel, and Lord's chi-square methods for item drift detection.* Paper presented at the National Council on Measurement in Education, Denver, CO.

Green, S. B., & Hershberger, S. L. (2000). Correlated errors in true score models and their effect on coefficient alpha. *Structural Equation Modeling, 7*(2), 251–270.

Gulliksen, H. (1950). *Theory of mental tests.* Hillsdale, NJ: Lawrence Erlbaum.

Guttman, L. (1945). A basis for analyzing test-retest reliability. *Psychometrika, 10*(4), 255–282.

Haebara, T. (1980). Equating logistic ability scales by a weighted least squares method. *Japanese Psychological Research, 22*(3), 144–149.

Hambleton, R. K., & Rodgers, J. H. (1995). Item bias review. *Practical Assessment, Research, and Evaluation, 4*(6). Retrieved from http://pareonline.net/getvn.asp?v=4&n=6

Hanson, B. A. (2002). IRT command language [Software].

Hanson, B. A., & Béguin, A. A. (2002). Obtaining a common scale for item response theory item parameters using separate versus concurrent estimation in the common-item equating design. *Applied Psychological Measurement, 26,* 3–24.

Hanson, B. A., & Brennan, R. L. (1990). An investigation of classification consistency indexes estimated under alternative strong true score models. *Journal of Educational Measurement, 27*(4), 345–359.

Holland, P. W., & Thayer, D. T. (1988). Differential item performance and the Mantel-Haenszel procedure. In H. Wainer & H. I. Braun (Eds.), *Test validity* (pp. 129–145). Hillsdale, NJ: Lawrence Erlbaum.

Huynh, H. (1976a). On the reliability of decisions in domain-referenced testing. *Journal of Educational Measurement, 13*(4), 253–264.

Huynh, H. (1976b). Statistical consideration of mastery scores. *Psychometrika, 41*(1), 65–78.

Huynh, H. (1996). Decomposition of a Rasch partial credit item into independent binary and indecomposable trinary items. *Psychometrika, 61*(1), 31–39.

Huynh, H. (2009, March 29). The golden numbers in Rasch linking protocol [Personal communication].

Huynh, H., & Meyer, J. P. (2003). Maximum information approach to scale description based on the Rasch model. *Journal of Applied Measurement, 4*, 101–110.

Huynh, H., & Meyer, J. P. (2010). Use of robust z in detecting unstable items in item response theory models. *Practical Assessment, Research and Evaluation, 15*(2), 1–8.

Jones, A. T. (2009). *Using the right tool for the job: An analysis of item selection statistics for criterion-referenced tests* (Doctoral dissertation). Available from ProQuest Dissertations and Theses database. (No. 3352760).

Jones, A. T. (2011). Comparing methods for item analysis: The impact of different item-selection statistics on test difficulty. *Applied Psychological Measurement, 35*(7), 566–571.

Jöreskog, K. G. (1971). Statistical analysis of sets of congeneric tests. *Psychometrika, 36*(2), 109–133.

Keats, J. A., & Lord, F. M. (1962). A theoretical distribution for mental test scores. *Psychometrika, 27*(1), 59–72.

Kim, S., & Kolen, M. J. (2007). Effects of scale linking on different definitions of criterion functions for the IRT characteristic curve methods. *Journal of Educational and Behavioral Statistics, 32*(4), 371–397.

Kim, S., & Lee, W.-C. (2006). An extension of four IRT linking methods for mixed-format tests. *Journal of Educational Measurement, 43*, 53–76.

Kolen, M. J. (2006). Scaling and norming. In R. L. Brennan (Ed.), *Educational measurement* (4th ed., 155–186). Westport, CT: Praeger.

Kolen, M. J., & Brennan, R. L. (2004). *Test equating, scaling, and linking: Methods and practices.* New York: Springer.

Kuder, G. F., & Richardson, M. W. (1937). Theory and estimation of test reliability. *Psychometrika, 2*(3), 151–160.

Lee, W.-C. (2007). Multinomial and compound multinomial error models for tests with complex item scoring. *Applied Psychological Measurement, 31*, 255–274. doi: 10.1177/0146621606294206

Lee, W.-C., Brennan, R. L., & Wan, L. (2009). Classification Consistency and Accuracy for Complex Assessments Under the Compound Multinomial Model. *Applied Psychological Measurement, 33*, 374–390. doi: 10.1177/0146621608321759

Linacre, J. M. (2012). *A user's guide to WINSTEPS and ministep Rasch model computer programs: Program manual 3.75.* Author.

Lord, F. M. (1952). The relation of the reliability of multiple-choice tests to the distribution of item difficulties. *Psychometrika, 17*, 181–194. doi: 10.1007/BF02288781

Lord, F. M. (1980). *Applications of item response theory to practical testing problems.* Hillsdale, NJ: Lawrence Erlbaum.

Lord, F. M., & Novick, M. R. (1968). *Statistical theories of mental test scores*. Reading, MA: Addison-Wesley.

Loyd, B. H., & Hoover, H. D. (1980). Vertical equating using the Rasch model. *Journal of Educational Measurement, 17*(3), 179–193.

Mantel, N. (1963). Chi-square tests with one degree of freedom; extensions of the Mantel-Haenszel procedure. *Journal of the American Statistical Association, 58*, 690–700.

Marco, G. L. (1977). Item characteristic curve solutions to three intractable testing problems. *Journal of Educational Measurement, 14*(2), 139–160.

Masters, G. N. (1982). A Rasch model for partial credit scoring. *Psychometrika, 47*(2), 149–174.

McDonald, R. P. (1999). *Test theory: A unified treatment*. Mahwah, NJ: Lawrence Erlbaum.

Meyer, J. P. (2010). *Reliability*. Oxford, United Kingdom: Oxford University Press.

Meyer, J. P., & Hailey, E. (2012). A study of Rasch partial credit, and rating scale model parameter recovery in WINSTEPS and jMetrik. *Journal of Applied Measurement, 13*(3), 248–258.

Meyer, J. P., & Huynh, H. (2010). *Evaluation of the robust z procedure for detecting item parameter drift in 3PLM and GPCM mixformat items*. Paper presented at the National Council on Measurement in Education, Denver, CO.

Muraki, E., & Bock, R. D. (2003). PARSCALE 4.1 [Computer program]. Chicago, IL: Scientific Software International.

Qualls, A. L. (1995). Estimating the reliability of a test containing multiple item formats. *Applied Measurement in Education, 8*(2), 111–120.

R Core Team. (2013). R: A Language and Environment for Statistical Computing [Software]. Vienna, Austria: R Foundation for Statistical Computing. Retrieved from www.R-project.org

Ramsay, J. O. (1991). Kernel smoothing approaches to nonparametric item characteristic curve estimation. *Psychometrika, 56*, 611–630.

Ramsay, J. O. (2000). TestGraf: A program for the graphical analysis of multiple choice test and questionnaire data [Computer program]. Montreal, Quebec: Author.

Rasch, G. (1977). On specific objectivity: An attempt at formalizing the request for generality and validity of scientific statements. *The Danish Yearbook of Philosophy, 14*, 58–93.

Rogers, H. J., & Swaminathan, H. (1990). Detecting differential item functioning using logistic regression procedures. *Journal of Educational Measurement, 27*, 361–370.

Rupp, A. A., & Zumbo, B. (2006). Understanding parameter invariance in unidimensional IRT models. *Educational and Psychological Measurement, 66*(1), 63–84. doi: 10.1177/0013164404273942

Spearman, C. (1904). The proof and measurement of association between two things. *American Journal of Psychology, 15*, 72–101.

Spearman, C. (1910). Correlation calculated from faulty data. *British Journal of Psychology, 3*, 271–295.

Stocking, M. L., & Lord, F. M. (1983). Developing a common metric in item response theory. *Applied Psychological Measurement, 7*(2), 201–210.

Subkoviak, M. J. (1976). Estimating reliability from a single administration of a criterion-referenced test. *Journal of Educational Measurement, 13*(4), 265–276.

Taherbhai, H., & Seo, D. (2013). The philosophical aspects of IRT equating: Modeling drift to evaluate cohort growth in large-scale assessments. *Educational Measurement: Issues and Practice, 32*, 2–14.

Thissen, D., & Steinberg, L. (1986). A taxonomy of item response models. *Psychometrika, 51*, 567–577.

Tong, Y., & Kolen, M. J. (2010). Scaling: An ITEMS module. *Educational Measurement: Issues and Practice, 29*, 39–48.

Uttaro, T., & Millsap, R. E. (1994). Factors influencing the Mantel-Haenszel procedure in the detection of differential item funcitoning. *Applied Psychological Measurement, 18*, 15–25.

Virginia Department of Education. (2012). *Virginia Standards of Learning Assessment Technical Report 2011–2012 Administration Cycle*. Richmond, VA: Virginia Department of Education.

Wainer, H., Bradlow, E. T., & Wang, X. (2007). *Testlet response theory and its applications*. New York, NY: Cambridge University Press.

Wells, C. S., Subkoviak, M. J., & Serlin, R. C. (2002). The effect of item parameter drift on examinee ability estimates. *Applied Psychological Measurement, 26*, 77–87.

Williams, P. E., Weiss, L. G., & Rolfhus, E. L. (2003). *WISC-IV technical report #2: Psychometric properties*. San Antonio, TX: Pearson.

Wilson, M. (1988). Detecting and interpreting item local dependence using a family of Rasch models. *Applied Psychological Measurement, 12*, 353–364.

Wilson, M. (2005). *Constructing measures*. Mahwah, NJ: Lawrence Erlbaum.

Wright, B., D., & Masters, G. N. (1982). *Rating scale analysis*. Chicago, IL: MESA Press.

Yen, W. M. (1984). Effects of local item dependence on the fit and equating performance of the three-parameter logistic model. *Applied Psychological Measurement, 8*, 125–145. doi: 10.1177/014662168400800201

Zimmerman, D. W., Zumbo, B., & LaLonde, C. (1993). Coefficient alpha as an estimate of reliability under violation of two assumptions. *Educational and Psychological Measurement, 53*, 33–49.

Zwick, R., & Ercikan, K. (1989). Analysis of differential item functioning in the NAEP history assessment. *Journal of Educational Measurement, 26*, 55–66.

Zwick, R., & Thayer, D. T. (1996). Evaluating the magnitude of differential item functioning in polytomous items. *Journal of Educational and Behavioral Statistics, 21*, 187–201.

INDEX

Printed by PGSTL